The Greenhaven Press
LITERARY COMPANION
to Contemporary Authors

TOM CLANCY

Richard Baiocco, *Book Editor*

Daniel Leone, *President*
Bonnie Szumski, *Publisher*
Scott Barbour, *Managing Editor*

**GREENHAVEN
PRESS ®**

THOMSON
—————*—————
GALE

San Diego • Detroit • New York • San Francisco • Cleveland
New Haven, Conn. • Waterville, Maine • London • Munich

© 2004 by Greenhaven Press. Greenhaven Press is an imprint of The Gale Group, Inc., a division of Thomson Learning, Inc.

Greenhaven® and Thomson Learning™ are trademarks used herein under license.

For more information, contact
Greenhaven Press
27500 Drake Rd.
Farmington Hills, MI 48331-3535
Or you can visit our Internet site at http://www.gale.com

Cover credit: © Kevin Fleming/CORBIS

LIBRARY OF CONGRESS CATALOGING-IN-PUBLICATION DATA

Readings on Tom Clancy / Richard Baiocco, book editor.
p. cm. — (The Greenhaven Press literary companion to contemporary authors)
Includes bibliographical references and index.
ISBN 0-7377-1743-2 (lib. bdg. : alk. paper) —
ISBN 0-7377-1744-0 (pbk. : alk. paper)
1. Clancy, Tom, 1947—Criticism and interpretation. 2. Adventure stories, American—History and criticism. 3. War stories, American—History and criticism. 4. Military art and science in literature. 5. Technology in literature. I. Baiocco, Richard. II. Series.
PS3553.L245Z85 2004
813'.54—dc21
2003041769

Printed in the United States of America

CONTENTS

Chapter 1: Clancy, Technology, and the Techno-Thriller

   Reviewers have credited Tom Clancy with inventing a
   new literary genre, the techno-thriller. In reality,
   Clancy's books share many characteristics with an
   older, established genre: science fiction.

   At the height of the Cold War Tom Clancy's techno-
   thrillers were finding a comfortable niche atop the
   best-seller lists. In this interview Clancy speaks can-
   didly about the two main ingredients of his novels:
   military heroes and technology.

Chapter 2: Reviews and Analyses of Tom Clancy's Major Works

   The Hunt for Red October launched Tom Clancy's
   career as an author of techno-thrillers. Critics feel that
   it is the accuracy of Clancy's perception of Soviet and
   American cultures that make this book such a success.

   Red Storm Rising is a successful and satisfying novel.

Clancy's descriptions of military hardware are technologically accurate, the plot is interesting, and his characters are likeable and engaging.

Chapter 3: In His Own Words

and Washington, D.C., Tom Clancy released this editorial to the press as a warning to whomever was responsible for the attacks. The message was clearly stated: The United States will have its revenge.

Chapter 4: Rebuilding an American Hero: The Appeal of Tom Clancy

popularity is his positive portrayal of America and American institutions. Clancy also presents positive male role models, a break from what has been fashionable since the early 1970s.

FOREWORD

Contemporary authors who earn millions of dollars writing best-sellers often face criticism that their work cannot be taken seriously as literature. For example, throughout most of his career, horror writer Stephen King has been dismissed by literary critics as a "hack" who writes grisly tales that appeal to the popular taste of the masses. Similarly, the extremely popular Harry Potter books by J.K. Rowling have been criticized as a clever marketing phenomenon that lack the imagination and depth of classic works of literature. Whether these accusations are accurate, however, remains debatable. As romance novelist Jayne Ann Krentz has pointed out:

> Popular fiction has been around forever but rarely has it been viewed as important in and of itself. Rarely have we acknowledged that it has a crucial place in culture. . . . The truth is, popular fiction—mysteries, science fiction, sword and sorcery, fantasy, glitz, romance, historical saga, horror, techno-thrillers, legal thrillers, forensic medical thrillers, serial killer thrillers, westerns, etc.—popular fiction is its own thing. It stands on its own. It draws its power from the ancient heroic traditions of storytelling—not modern angst. It is important, even if it is entertaining.

Although its importance often goes unrecognized, popular fiction has the power to reach millions of readers and to thus influence culture and society. The medium has the potential to shape culture because of the large and far-flung audience that is drawn to read these works. As a result of their large readership, contemporary authors have a unique venue in which to reflect and explore the social and political issues that they find important. Far from being mere escapist fiction, their works often address topics that challenge readers to consider their perspectives on current and universal themes. For example, Michael Crichton's novel *Jurassic Park*, while an entertaining if disturbing story about what could happen if dinosaurs roamed the planet today, also explores the potential negative consequences of scientific advances and the ethical issues of DNA experimentation. Similarly, in his 1994 novel *Disclosure*, Crichton tells the story of a man who suffers predatory sexual harassment by his female supervisor. By reversing the expected genders of the victim and aggressor, Crichton added fuel to the debate over sexual politics in the workplace.

Some works of fiction are compelling and popular because they address specific concerns that are prevalent in a culture at a given time. For example, John Grisham has written numerous novels about the theme of corruption in America's oldest legal and business institutions. In books such as *The Firm* and *The Pelican Brief*, courageous though sometimes naive individuals must confront established, authoritarian systems at great personal danger in order to bring the truth to light. Written at a time when government and corporate scandals dominated the headlines, his novels reflect a faith in the power of the individual to achieve justice.

In an era when 98 percent of American households have a television and annual video sales outnumber book sales, it is impossible to ignore the fact that popular fiction also inspires people to read. The Harry Potter stories have been enormously popular with both adults and children, setting records on the *New York Times* best-seller lists. Stephen King's books, which have never gone out of print, frequently occupy four to five shelves in bookstores and libraries. Although literary critics may find fault with some works of popular fiction, record numbers of people are finding value in reading these contemporary authors whose stories hold meaning for them and which shape popular culture.

Greenhaven Press's Literary Companion to Contemporary Authors series is designed to provide an introduction to the works of modern authors. Each volume profiles a different author. A biographical essay sets the stage by tracing the author's life and career. Next, each anthology in the series contains a varied selection of essays that express diverse views on the author under discussion. A concise introduction that presents the contributing writers' main themes and insights accompanies each selection. Essays, profiles, and reviews offer in-depth biographical information, analysis of the author's predominant themes, and literary analysis of the author's trademark books. In addition, primary sources such as interviews and the author's own essays and writings are included wherever possible. A comprehensive index and an annotated table of contents help readers quickly locate material of interest. In order to facilitate further research, each title includes a bibliography of the author's works and books about the author's writing and life. These features make Greenhaven Press's Literary Companion to Contemporary Authors series ideal for readers interested in literary analysis on the world's modern authors and works.

INTRODUCTION: TAPPING INTO PATRIOTISM

Tom Clancy's career is the stuff of fantasy. When *Time* magazine quoted then-president Ronald Reagan in 1984 as saying *The Hunt for Red October* was "the perfect yarn," insurance salesman-turned-author Tom Clancy's spectacular conquest of the nation's best-seller lists began. The culmination of Clancy's popularity came when Putnam's Sons offered Clancy $45 million for a two-book contract nearly a decade and a half later, making him one of the highest-paid writers ever.

With more than 30 million books in print, Tom Clancy is one of the most popular authors in history. Although other writers of mass-market fiction, such as Stephen King, Danielle Steele, or John Grisham, may have similar book sales, Tom Clancy has demonstrated that he is more than just a fabulously successful author. In addition to four of his novels having been transformed into mega-blockbuster movies, Clancy's multimedia company, Red Storm Entertainment, is creating some of the best-selling military simulation video games on the market, galvanizing the attention of an entirely new generation that was not even alive when Clancy's first novel was published. Clancy has also authored a respectable list of nonfiction books, such as *Into the Storm: A Study in Command, Airborne, Carrier, Marine,* and *SSN: Strategies of Submarine Warfare,* which have garnered high praise from critics for their technical accuracy and Clancy's ability to convey complex material in a lucid and engaging narrative.

What is it about Tom Clancy's novels that have made the

writer such a tremendous success? By celebrating the extreme bravery and courage that members of the U.S. military demonstrate, Clancy has been able to tap into a sense of patriotism that is deeply held by millions of Americans. The author writes passionately about men and women who serve in the military and conveys to his readers his deeply held belief that they are worthy of respect. Moreover, Clancy's accurate descriptions of technologically sophisticated weaponry give his books a credibility that many of his imitators lack.

As is often the case with a literary phenomenon, Tom Clancy's success has created a critical backlash. Although all of Clancy's novels have graced the top spots on the *New York Times* best-seller list, some critics dismiss Clancy as a wholly average writer whose works feature formulaic plotlines and one-dimensional characters, and who relies too heavily on loyal followers who will read, play, or watch anything with the author's name on it. Many critics take particular exception to Clancy's creation of the "Op-Center" in 1995 that consisted of a team of writers who authored books based on plot sketches proposed by Clancy. These books sold and continue to sell well to the public, but critics have voiced consternation about the author's "corporatization" of the creative process.

A large part of Tom Clancy's success can be attributed to his creation of the heroic character Jack Ryan, the morally upright, courageous protagonist of many of Clancy's novels. Clancy portrays Ryan as an intelligent, wealthy, well-married man who has the confidence to take risks and handle potentially catastrophic situations without cracking. At the beginning of *The Hunt for Red October*, Clancy writes that Ryan could not be bought, bribed, or bullied because he came from money and was married to more money. For Clancy, and for many of his readers, Jack Ryan fulfills the fantasy of fiscal independence that allows for personal freedom and self-assurance. For Clancy and his readers, Jack Ryan is an icon—both symbol and defender of their most closely held values.

THE LIFE OF THOMAS L. CLANCY

Thomas L. Clancy was born on April 12, 1947, in Baltimore, Maryland, the son of a mailman who had served in the U.S. Navy. Tom's father, he recalls, "taught me to be independent." Tom's mother worked in the credit department for Montgomery Ward, a department store chain, to earn the tuition to send him to parochial school. Educated by Jesuits, Tom recalls having had ethics pounded into him.

As a teenager, Tom was fascinated by gadgets. He was absolutely in awe of the idea of manned spaceflight. Tom was also fascinated with military history and spent most of his time reading about the weaponry used in World Wars I and II. By his own admission, Tom was a lazy student, as his subpar grades indicated. Those low marks, however, concealed Tom's curiosity and willingness to educate himself.

Looking to follow in his father's footsteps, Tom tried to join the military services following high school, but the six-foot-two-inch, one-hundred-eighty-pound teenager was rejected because he was severely nearsighted. Tom settled for the ROTC program at Loyola, where he enrolled as a freshman in 1965. Much to Clancy's dismay, his poor eyesight forced him out of the ROTC program. With the Vietnam War raging, Clancy was crushed because he felt he would have made an excellent tank commander. Instead, Clancy finished his education at Loyola in June 1969, graduating with a B.A. in English. Two months later, Clancy married a nursing student named Wanda Thomas.

To support himself and Wanda, Clancy took a job selling insurance. He worked as an agent in Baltimore, Maryland,

and in Hartford, Connecticut, until 1973. At that point, the Clancys moved to Owings, Maryland, where he took a permanent job for the O.F. Bowen Agency. The agency was owned by Wanda's grandparents, but Clancy was also a talented agent. His list of clients grew to more than eleven hundred, and in 1980 Clancy was able to buy the company.

Despite his success, Tom Clancy never felt that the life of a businessman was stimulating enough for him. In interviews he has been quoted as saying that selling insurance was not "intellectually satisfying," and although he was able to pay the bills, he felt restless with such an ordinary, routine job. Clancy yearned for a career that would catapult him out on his own and give him a more concrete sense of worth and prosperity than the selling of insurance could offer.

Clancy recalled an early teenage ambition of seeing his name on a book cover in the Library of Congress. With a goal firmly in mind, Clancy worked to develop plots for political and military thrillers. He was particularly intrigued and inspired by the true story of a Soviet missile frigate, the *Storozhedoy*, and its failed attempt to defect from Latvia to the Swedish island of Gotland in 1975. The ship's political officer, Valeri Sablin, was captured, court-martialed and executed. The story percolated in Clancy's mind for years before he finally had the confidence to write a novel inspired by this incident.

RED OCTOBER

In 1982 Tom Clancy began researching and writing the novel that would be published as *The Hunt for Red October.* Although he had been creating plots in his head for years, Clancy recalls that the day he began writing *The Hunt for Red October* was the day "the muse kissed me." In Clancy's story, Soviet captain first rank Marko Ramius successfully defects to the United States, not in a frigate but in a new, state-of-the-art submarine, the *Red October.* What made Clancy's novel different from others in the thriller genre was the amount of highly accurate technical detail he included.

Whereas most writers only described the workings of military hardware in general terms, Clancy portrayed the precise activities of men operating such equipment.

Seven nights a week Clancy would drag the typewriter home from his insurance office and convert his family's dining room table into a study. There, he would type furiously the novel that he had been mapping in his head ever since he had heard the story of the *Storozhedoy.* The process was exciting and satisfied his creative impulses, but at the same time it was demanding. After six months of writing every night, Tom Clancy finished the first draft of *The Hunt for Red October.*

Tom Clancy's research for *Red October* did not come from top-secret classified U.S. Navy files, as some who read his book believed, but rather from two books, Norman Polmar's *Guide to the Soviet Navy* and *Combat Fleets of the World,* as well as a war simulation game called *Harpoon.* The books and the game were all readily available to the public. Clancy also sought the help of a former submariner with a doctorate in physics named Ralph Chatham, who taught Clancy how submariners spoke and gave him tips on the tenseness of life below sea level. For his efforts, Chatham earned the dedication in what would be Clancy's debut novel.

With a first draft of his novel completed, Clancy began the arduous task of looking for a publisher. Wanda began to worry when all the major publishing companies passed on the soon-to-be best-selling author's first novel. She constantly reminded her husband that they were not so financially sound from the insurance business that his attention could be so supremely occupied with this book. Clancy persisted despite his wife's concerns, polishing his manuscript as he continued to search for a publisher. Part of Clancy's problem was that he was unknown to those who publish fiction. The only things Clancy had printed were an editorial and a three-page article on MX missiles in the Naval Institute Press's monthly magazine.

The Naval Institute Press is the publishing arm of the Naval Institute and is primarily a scholarly publisher responsible for printing manuals such as *The Bluejackets' Manual,* which serves as a basic reference for all naval personnel from seaman to admiral. Although the institute had never published fiction before, Clancy submitted *The Hunt for Red October* to the Naval Institute Press on February 28, 1983, more out of hope that someone there would suggest where else he might send his manuscript than with any thought that the institute would actually publish it. The Naval Institute Press, however, offered Clancy a $5,000 advance and agreed to publish it if he rewrote the manuscript.

Clancy was proud of his accomplishment but remained humble. He asked Wanda if she thought the manuscript would sell five thousand copies and was astonished when she replied that she thought it would sell more like fifty thousand copies. When *The Hunt for Red October* was finally published, in October 1984, it achieved modest sales of some fourteen thousand copies. At the time, however, Clancy was just glad to have his name on the cover of a book. Both he and Wanda knew that to reach the level of bestseller, however, it would take luck and publicity.

"A Perfect Yarn"

That luck and publicity came in the form of a favorable assessment from one of the most influential men in the world: U.S. president Ronald Reagan. The publication of *Red October* had created quite a stir in the military, especially at OP-02, the headquarters for the navy's submarine operations. Officials there expressed consternation over what many believed was a serious breach of secrecy since Clancy had managed to make extremely accurate guesses regarding the navy's submarine tactics and strategy. Many naval officials believed that Clancy must have had access to classified naval documents as he wrote his novel. In the midst of the controversy, President Reagan decided to read the novel himself. After he finished the book he declared to *Time* magazine that *The Hunt for Red October* was "the perfect yarn."

The president's positive response was just the break Clancy needed. After Reagan's comment became public, the book soon made it onto the *New York Times* best-seller list. Clancy was astonished by how quickly the transformation from insurance agent writing part-time for an obscure publisher to best-selling author was accomplished. He described the process in one word: "Boom!" Although being a best-selling novelist brought Tom Clancy financial security, he and Wanda continued to work in their insurance business. In fact, not until 1987 did Clancy officially stop working at the insurance agency.

At age thirty-seven, Tom Clancy was finally able—vicariously—to fulfill his dream of being a soldier by writing about military men and the lives they lead. His fame as the author of *Red October* opened up many doors in the world of the military. He began receiving invitations to speak at naval conferences. Clancy also was granted unprecedented access to a submarine and its crew since the navy saw in Tom Clancy and his fiction a new means of boosting its public image.

HITTING HIS STRIDE

In 1986 Tom Clancy followed up the success of *Red October* with *Red Storm Rising*, a book he cowrote with a former naval intelligence operative, Larry Bond. *Red Storm Rising* deals with the scenario of how World War III could start. In the book, the Soviet Union, seeking to divert the West's attention from plans to take over oil fields, invades West Germany. What set *Red Storm Rising* apart from most political-military thrillers was that it dealt with a nonnuclear confrontation, whereas most novelists were obsessed with the prospects and consequences of nuclear war. Tom Clancy had no problem gaining firsthand knowledge of military operations as he prepared to write *Red Storm Rising*. The navy put him aboard a frigate for a week to learn about antisubmarine warfare.

For *Red Storm Rising* Tom Clancy signed on with Putnam's

Sons, much to the dismay of the Naval Institute Press. Putnam offered him an advance of $1 million. Clancy and Bond split the advance, although Putnam kept Bond's name off the book's cover, making it clear that they wanted to make the most of Clancy's popularity.

Some critics praised *Red Storm Rising*, saying that it was a testimonial to Clancy's skill as a writer. Others, however, contended that Clancy "sanitized" war by failing to depict the true carnage a conflict in Western Europe would involve.

Clancy also came under fire for a tendency to overplay the efficiency of the weapons he described during the war. Most military veterans will argue that weapons rarely work as neatly as Clancy envisions them to.

Critics' objections notwithstanding, *Red Storm Rising* was very well received by the public, selling well over a million copies. What made this success even sweeter was that it meant Clancy had beaten the dreaded "sophomore jinx," the tendency of new authors' second books to fail miserably. *Red October*, the book-buying public now knew, was not a fluke.

In 1987 Clancy brought back one of his heroes from *Red October*, Jack Ryan, in his third novel, *Patriot Games*. This time, the villains were not Soviets but rather terrorists from a splinter group of the Irish Republican Army. In the novel, Ryan defeats the terrorists after they attack his home, where he is playing host to members of the British royal family.

A LESS-POSITIVE RECEPTION

Patriot Games proved less successful than Clancy's previous efforts. Some critics attribute the less-positive reception to Clancy's effort to focus more on the Ryan family than on military and political themes. Critics also noted that in the majority of Clancy's sweeping techno-thrillers, he employs broadly drawn, somewhat vague characters to drive the plot, but in *Patriot Games* this strategy was ineffective in helping portray the dynamics within the Ryan family.

The following year Clancy produced *The Cardinal of the*

Kremlin, a spy novel dealing with satellite-based lasers that could prevent nuclear attacks by taking out nuclear missle silos from space. Clancy claims that the character of the cardinal, a senior officer in the Soviet intelligence service who is secretly aiding the United States, was conceptualized while he was working on an early draft of *The Hunt for Red October*. Clancy felt that the character was interesting enough to save and develop later.

With the publication of *Kremlin*, and Clancy's well-publicized visits to various military locations, rumors again spread that he was disclosing classified information. This was a time when America's military planners were first seriously considering an orbital defense against nuclear attack—a program known as the Strategic Defense Initiative (SDI). Clancy vehemently denied all such allegations, but concern heightened to the point that the CIA asked Clancy either not to mention the laser in his manuscript or not publish the book altogether. Once again, Clancy was able to prove that he had obtained all the information from publicly available sources. Those who know Clancy's research techniques, in fact, compare them to those used by a competent KGB agent—that is, he searches publicly available documents with great thoroughness, extracting the information he needs.

Tom Clancy closed the decade of the 1980s with *Clear and Present Danger* (1989), a continuation of the Jack Ryan series that deals with two topics that dominated the news media at that time. The first was the scourge of illicit drugs that seemed to be pouring into the country, and the other was the infamous attempt to funnel covert aid to Nicaraguan counterrevolutionaries, a scandal known as the Iran-contra affair. Clancy blended these two topics to create a fictitious account of an American war on the importation of cocaine from Colombia. As the novel unfolds, a conspiracy similar to Iran-contra is exposed, and Clancy's novel becomes an examination of the use and abuse of the political and military power by public officials.

Clear and Present Danger went on to be the highest-selling book of the 1980s, and as the new decade began, Tom Clancy found himself consistently sitting on top of the *New York Times* best-seller list with a following that was so loyal it seemed to read anything bearing his name.

A HOLLYWOOD GEM

Clancy's success in the world of mass-market literature led to many offers for movie adaptations of his books and made Tom Clancy a hot commodity in Hollywood. The screen adaptation of *The Hunt for Red October*, starring Sean Connery and Alec Baldwin, came out in 1990 and was an immediate hit. *Patriot Games* came out in 1992, and despite the problems with the book, the film was a monumental success. *Clear and Present Danger* came out in 1994. The popularity of Tom Clancy made the leading role in a Jack Ryan film something big stars coveted.

Although moviegoers loved the screen adaptations of Clancy's techno-thrillers, Clancy himself has voiced mixed feelings about Hollywood. The author acknowledges that all the films based on his books have been well received by audiences and have made him a substantial amount of money, but he has concerns over the way screenwriters introduce factual errors that are not present in his books.

For example, according to Clancy, the screen version of *The Hunt for Red October* lacked the technical accuracy regarding the submarine's size and its weaponry—something that he tried to convey faithfully in the novel. At the same time, Clancy recognizes that the printed word and the visual representation on the screen are two different art forms and that sacrifices, such as the technical aspect of the novels, must be made so as not to impede the flow of the on-screen action.

The latter half of the 1990s was a productive time for Tom Clancy, in part because he relinquished the role of writer in favor of a less-direct creative role. In 1995 Clancy, with his friend Steve Pieczenik, created the "Op-Center," which consisted of a team of writers who authored books based on basic ideas proposed by Clancy. Some of the books were *Mission of Honor, Acts of War,* and *Balance of Power.* In 2002 a three-volume set of all the Op-Center books was released. Many observers criticized Clancy for such an assembly-line approach to fiction and predicted that Clancy would discredit himself as a writer. Clancy, however, continued to write his own novels throughout the 1990s as well, in the process demonstrating that he had not lost his creative touch.

Clancy also created the Guided Tours series, which were essentially nonfiction technical descriptions of the inner workings of various military units or weapon systems. He wrote *Submarines* (1993), *Armored Warfare* (1994), *Fighter Wing* (1995), *Marine* (1996), and *Airborne* (1997). The Guided Tours series served as a good venue for Clancy to demonstrate his affinity for and skill at writing on technical topics.

Another branch of the Clancy franchise formed in November 1996 when he and the Virtus Corporation founded Red Storm Entertainment to create and market multiple-media entertainment products. Red Storm Entertainment released its first game, *Politika,* in November 1997, and it was the first online game ever packaged with a mass-market paperback book.

In March 1998 Tom extended the Clancy empire still further by making a $200 million bid to buy the Minnesota Vikings of the National Football League (NFL). Clancy liked the idea of having a team operating beneath his control, and with the income he was making, the bid did not seem so far-fetched. Unfortunately for Clancy, despite signing a two-book contract with his publisher, Penguin Putnam, for an unprecedented $45 million, the author was forced to drop his NFL bid that May for financial reasons.

Meanwhile, Clancy still found time to write *Without Remorse* (1993), *Debt of Honor* (1994), *Executive Orders* (1996), *Into the Storm* (1997), and *Rainbow Six* (1998). All of these books spent time at or near the top of the *New York Times* best-seller list.

In *Debt of Honor* and *Executive Orders*, Clancy speculates on the idea of America being ruined by a foreign terrorist attack yet retaining the grace and strength to rebuild itself. In *Debt of Honor* readers learn that after a few years away from the CIA, Jack Ryan is asked to come back as national security adviser to the president, who is receiving threats from Japan of a possible invasion. The book, however, was panned by some critics as Japan-bashing.

Executive Orders begins where *Debt of Honor* leaves off. In the novel, a jumbo jet has crashed into the capitol, and the president, the cabinet, and most of Congress have been killed. It is up to Jack Ryan, who has been elected vice president, to ward off adversaries looking to capitalize on America's misfortunes.

CLANCY THROUGH THE MILLENNIUM

Before the millennium closed, Tom Clancy filed for divorce from his wife, Wanda, in July 1998 after nearly thirty years of marriage. Clancy was appreciative of Wanda's support when he first began writing, but his fame took him away from his family for weeks at a time as he traveled to promote his books and give lectures. Following the divorce, Clancy began being seen in public and at various conferences accompanied by various girlfriends. Clancy let it be known that he expected to soon be married again.

Clancy continued to make Red Storm Entertainment a priority, and in the years since *Politika* came out, he has released a number of military simulation video games that have built on his initial success. In the literary world, however, techno-thriller writers were facing a serious problem, and Clancy was no exception. The Cold War was over, and critics were wondering if writers like Clancy, whose books usually cast the Soviet Union in the role of evildoer, would be able to create believable stories in a world without Soviet-American competition.

One solution Clancy tried in his 2002 release, *Red Rabbit*, was to set the clocks back twenty years to 1981 and imagine how the KGB might have been behind the attempted assassination that year of Pope John Paul II. Such a scenario was given added credibility by the fact that the KGB had already been implicated in the actual attempt on the pope's life. However, for fans and critics alike who agreed that one of Tom Clancy's strengths was being on the fringe of new technology and modern warfare, *Red Rabbit* came off as if he had simply recycled an old, previously abandoned manuscript.

The Bear and the Dragon, another novel in which Jack Ryan is the U.S. president, has been similarly criticized. Jack Ryan faces problems with China, but with its many undertones of a subversive KGB connection, the novel was poorly received. Critics cited the novel's failure to be cutting edge and distance itself convincingly from the Cold War. Clancy has defended his approach, saying that the Cold War is still a viable topic for writers of fiction, just as World War II has been for decades.

One problem Clancy has alluded to is the difficulty of creating fiction that competes with real life. Tom Clancy has stated that with the terrorist attacks on America on September 11, 2001, the plots he and fellow writers come up with are no longer shocking. Regardless of the response to his latest efforts, fifty-five-year-old Clancy says he has no plans to stop writing. Tom Clancy's contribution to mass-market fiction is undeniable, and although critics find it no problem to pick apart Clancy's skill as a writer, his ability to entertain can stand atop his astronomical book sales. Just the sheer number of products that his name is attached to is a testament to his success.

THE IMPORTANCE OF TOM CLANCY

Throughout his career, Tom Clancy has remained a literary conundrum among critics. While certain Clancy detractors cite the baseness of his stereotypical characters, his blind patriotism, his inability or unwillingness to incorporate sex into his novels, and his failure to deal with the subject of love in any depth, Clancy continues to have a devoted following. He has well over 30 million books in print, which not only makes him one of America's most popular authors but also one of the world's most popular.

For his part, Clancy continues to see his greatest contribution as restoring a measure of public faith in a military establishment that had previously seen its reputation sullied by America's defeat in Vietnam. Tom Clancy has dedicated his professional writing career to portraying the sacrifices made by courageous men and women of the U.S. military. Clancy feels inspired by these soldiers and considers it his duty to portray their heroics as accurately as possible. For their part, military officials agree that Clancy has done a remarkable job of countering some of the criticism that was directed toward the military in the last decades of the twentieth century. America's military leaders say that by recognizing and accurately depicting the bravery and sacrifice made by the members of the armed forces, Tom Clancy is rendering a service to his country.

CHAPTER 1

Clancy, Technology, and the Techno-Thriller

The Techno-Thriller and Its Origin

William F. Ryan

William F. Ryan argues that despite the author's denials that he writes techno-thrillers, Tom Clancy pioneered this type of fiction. Ryan asserts that the techno-thriller shares two characteristics with science fiction. The first is that the plot always involves the use of advanced technology for waging war. The second characteristic is stereotypical characters who lack personal complexities that might impede the flow of the narrative.

The late William F. Ryan was a journalist and his interviews with famous authors such as Norman Mailer and James Michener were regularly featured in *Virginia Quarterly Review* in the ten years preceding his death.

Tom Clancy became a writer of big books. Hefty novels for summer beaches or those long airline flights to spots where Clancy never goes. His first, *The Hunt for Red October*, arrived for sale in late 1984. Clancy's stars were clearly in place for Christmas. The publisher was the U.S. Naval Institute Press. Clancy's first book was the Institute's first gambit at publishing original fiction. It caught good attention in official Washington, D.C. Here at last was a fresh new thriller for career professionals in the Defense Department. Some important people in the State Department's diplomatic corps read the book and passed it around. The novel was mentioned at parties. A copy was placed under the White House Christmas tree. Not long after New Year's 1985, President

William F. Ryan, "The Genesis of the Techno-Thriller," *The Virginia Quarterly Review*, Winter 1993, pp. 24–40. Copyright © 1993 by *The Virginia Quarterly Review*. Reproduced by permission.

Ronald Reagan told a *Time* interviewer that *Red October* is "the perfect yarn."

Only a few have questioned that praise. The book has no doubt carved a niche in cultural history as a phenomenon of the 1980's. It proved to be a pace setter for Clancy's further authorship and an impressive model to all Clancy disciples and imitators. This was the new way into big bucks from books. Surely this was a business after all. . . . Or was it?

William S. Burroughs once asserted to me that every novelist writes as well as he or she can. He means that all writers produce at the peak of their skills or forms no matter what they say to seminars or interviewers.. In the end, the collective aim of Melville, Faulkner, Kerouac, Mickey Spillane, and Iceberg Slim has been to earn two or three squares a day by one's pen. So if it's a business, it has some integrity.

The phenomenology of Clancy and devotees in his train occurs in literary circles. What spurred this discussion was the quick-draw jargon or newspeak of those three-minute oracles who review books for the mass media. I remain unwilling to call those persons critics. But their mission is to pinpoint trends, fads, shifts in the psychotic American breeze. By the late 1980's, one or more of them were calling Tom Clancy the wizard inventor of the *techno-thriller*.

To accept this blurb as literary history is to admit that Clancy created a new genre fiction. When his *Red October* and *Red Storm Rising* (Putnam, 1986) were published, no one else seemed to be writing or even talking about his kind of novel. Then came Stephen Coonts with *Flight of the Intruder* (U.S. Naval Institute Press, 1986) and Harold Coyle with *Team Yankee: A Novel of World War III* (Presidio Press, 1987). In short order a battalion of mimickers brought up the rear. Their colors are brazen and evident. . . .

CHARACTERISTICS OF THE TECHNO-THRILLER

The techno-thrillers stand tall and thick in bookstores. The paperback renderings shimmer with glossy inks (good for reading in foxholes and duck blinds) and comic book graphics. The stories ring with patriotic fervor and a Manichean discernment of good versus evil. You always know your enemies. You quickly spot the good guys. You know from the outset which side will win because destiny commands it. These books are the proving grounds and playing fields of a warrior class. Heroes abound in the stories, most of them soldiers, seamen, fighter pilots, military officers, spies, or other mavens of espionage. The novels are just long enough to become variously exciting, laborious, and silly. The plots and crucial sequences always rely on advanced technology for waging war. This quality of the techno-thriller links it to science fiction. Remember that or underline it. What annoys many readers is that such SF [science fiction] purists as Isaac Asimov and James E. Gunn sacrifice character development for scientific explication in their stories. The techno-thriller makes a similar sacrifice much of the time and mounts a paradox. Heroes and other soldiers are game pieces, mannequins, cardboard stand-ups in a showroom window. They have all the human complexity and élan of the Blackhawks or Batman and Robin of the World War II comic books. In inverse proportion, the Soviet enemies, terrorists, and other villains are sculpted to deliver character traits and singular menace. This is the case in all of Clancy's published novels to date.

My initial supposition about the audience for these books was that only the techno-freaks attached to research and development firms, or troops in "Ollie's Army [an examination of the grass roots support behind Oliver North's historic 1994 Virginia Senate Campaign]," would ever buy them. Those are in fact the true zealots. But much of the English-reading world has ingested works of this genre. C.S. Forester's "Hornblower" series and George MacDonald Fraser's "Flashman" frolics have now been outclassed—for now, at least—by Clancy's chronicles of Jack Ryan. I was bound to be curious sooner or later. With a lot of bothersome questions, I first approached Tom Clancy, and later, his friend Stephen Coonts.

THE ANTI-TECHNO-THRILLER WRITER

If there is a new genre, Clancy denies any connection with it. He insists that he writes novels, and they are thrillers. To make much more of it is to test his anger. He referred to Michael Crichton's big seller, *The Andromeda Strain* (Knopf, 1969). "If anybody invented the techno-thriller, what about Crichton, when I was in college? All you're doing is describing tools used by your characters. Technology is another word for tools."

The matter of Clancy's characters and how they function is a short subject made long by engaging the author in debate. He believes that he's done an exemplary job. His reinforcement comes from "people in the business" who read his books right on time and comment that what he does well is "capture the personalities." But what business is he talking about? The genre fiction that used to be just for newsstand pulps? What people in what business?

Not long after reading Clancy's *The Cardinal of the Kremlin* (Putnam, 1988), I got hold of a short story he had published in a high school literary magazine. Its title is "The Wait." Printed in 1965, it indexes the personality of a teenager who's patriotic and fine-tuned to world affairs. His concerns then are his concerns now. Clancy loathes revolutionaries and guerrillas, most likely because they flout the law. He emulates the tough, faceless soldier who puts his life on the line against Communism. "The Wait" is precisely the same schmaltz on a sub roll that he's been packaging for "thrillers" ever since. If Clancy refuses to own up to the techno-thriller, he might grant instead that he has given us five or six national security Westerns. The cowpokes wear black shoes and know how to fight showdowns with computers. Those are Clancy's people. Their business may not be for our eyes and ears. But trust Clancy.

He told me of a conversation from 1987, when he and his family visited England a second time. "A friend of mine was the skipper of H.M.S. *Boxer*, a frigate," he said. "We were having lunch in his stateroom aboard. He looked at me and he said, 'Tom, the technology in your books is not terribly impressive, but I think the characters are bloody accurate.' I wanted to grab him by the throat and say, 'Why don't you tell the God-damned critics?' But the people in the business tell me that the technology is no big deal, because any fool can do that. What I do well is capture the personalities."

What I've heard and read is just the reverse. Clancy has prodigious facility with high technology but his characters are tilting scarecrows. His third novel, *Patriot Games* (1987), deals less with war technology than with law enforcement and shooting it out with urban guerrillas. When we spoke, he said he regards this novel as his finest. Most reviews faulted this book more than his others, and on the same grounds. Only he and those "people in the business" have kind words for his characters. But the book sold extremely well as usual. Clancy need not defend himself.

In conversation with him I pushed the issue of his characters, perhaps a bit too far. I asked, for example, whether Prince Charles had shown any reaction to Clancy's portrayal of him in *Patriot Games*.

"No more than President Reagan had a reaction to the fact that there's a president in *Red October, Red Storm* and *Cardinal*," he said: "He was a generic character. He was never intended to be Charles, Prince of Wales. He's just a character. If in any American political thriller novel you have a president, you don't necessarily mean President Reagan or President Ford or President Carter. You just mean a person who has the job. I simply treated the Prince of Wales as the same sort of literary invention. If you pay close attention there are enough clues to tell you that it's not Charles."

Again, please take note. The techno-thriller is bound to be inhabited by *generic* characters. Once the reader has expended those brain cells in processing data on machineries of devastation, he is perhaps amenable to drastic suspensions of disbelief. The existence of parallel worlds, for example. The one on which we walk, eat meals, read books, watch television, and gratefully go to sleep. The other is for Clancy's callow Prince, his renderings of nameless U.S. presidents who attain to dullness and stupidity, a martinet national security advisor named Jeffrey Pelt, a CIA director known as Judge Moore. Men with jobs. With each big book we get a cigar box full of tin men with guns. In the usual course of things, Clancy's women are as wan and insipid as tea left standing for three days. Clancy's recurring hero is Jack Ryan, very square and very opaque. With every book Jack's ties to the CIA are tighter. He advances upward, gets richer. The nation relies on him more and more. He could run for Congress if we ever knew anything meaningful about him.

Clancy insisted more than once that he writes about a "generic category of *hero.*" The idea by itself is specious outside the comic books. All the same, the legions of devotees who read his novels have not diminished. He tells a good story, spins an exciting yarn. The characters don't accomplish a thing in the techno-thriller. They generate no electricity. They are understood only by what they do. Their definition is the purpose of their mission.

Readers of this genre fiction are apt to find escapist fun but little or no artistry. Clancy told me that he thinks of himself as an entertainer with no pretense to literary matters or concerns. In my own fashion I looked for a durable message in the works of Tom Clancy. He often denies that he ever intends any such thing. But I asked anyway. In all those Cold War potboilers, isn't Clancy saying that there are ways to wage *peace* through a new balance of power in the world?

"You may be right," he answered. "As Claudius Appius the Blind said, '*Si vis pacem parate pro bellum.* . . . If you desire peace, prepare for war.' The other thing I say in there is that people we have wearing uniforms and carrying badges are important members of our society and entitled to respect. They don't have halos. You may not always want your daughter to go out and date one. But we should treat them decently because they're out there for us. The Pentagon Navy is not the same as the fleet Navy. I know that. And that may find its way into my next book."

OTHER TECHNO-THRILLER WRITERS

Following the success of his *Team Yankee*, Harold Coyle wrote *Sword Point* (1988) and *Bright Star* (1990), both techno-thrillers from Simon & Schuster. Coyle is a friend to Tom Clancy, as is Stephen Coonts. After his *Flight of the Intruder*, Coonts encored with *Final Flight* (Doubleday, 1988), then *The Minotaur* (Doubleday, 1989) and *Under Siege* (Pocket Books, 1990). Standing in Clancy's long shadow is no encumbrance for the other two. They are where they are because Clancy was the pathfinder. But I paid special attention to Coonts because of his rather different style and approach to a story. . . .

Coonts draws on classical mythology to shape his stories. Ovid's *Metamorphoses* has long been his source book. But he also told me that *Flight of the Intruder* is largely based on the Biblical story of Job. The hero of his novels is fighter pilot Jake Grafton, a battle-tough counterpart of Clancy's Jack Ryan. In this first novel, Jake is up against temptations of hubris, vengeance, and reckless disregard for human lives.

ART VS. ENTERTAINMENT

Coonts talked about how he became a novelist. "A man is scared and shot at and changed," he said. "If he comes home alive he finds a new zest in life. He sees things as others do not. He deals with timeless conflicts of the human condition. You're on solid ground as a storyteller if you take new approaches to man's duty to society and to other human beings. Stories should try to captivate but not preach or give answers." In Coonts I would say the key word is changed. . . .

Those are lofty ideals, all right. Stendhal [French writer who chronicled life in France after Napoléon] might have vocalized them, or Ernest Hemingway [American expatriot writer] during breakfast. Do they apply to the techno-thriller? Some years ago, metacritics and a few popular novelists wrote and lectured on *moral fiction.* Where are those debates today? The techno-thriller and its practitioners may be standing athwart. Tom Clancy, for one, made it clear to me that he has no interest in contemporary literature as *Literature.* He perennially scorns any salon environs. He spoke of the legendary Algonquin [famous group of writers who met at the Algonquin hotel in the mid 1920s] Round Table in pejoratives. Never studied the modern novel as a course, never took creative writing in a school setting. . . .

[Coonts] credits Tom Clancy with rescuing the story of the hero in uniform and making it shine. After a long lapse the publishers could sell those swagger-and-salvo books in high volume. It isn't corn and camp any longer. So says Stephen Coonts. He looks back at 20 years of American fiction and sees the military image scarred by Vietnam recoil. The man in uniform was often painted as psychopathic, perverted, and criminal. But didn't the splendid novels of James Webb accomplish this revision years before the techno-thriller? Not as Coonts reads the flow chart. Jim Webb writes best sellers but they don't reap the rewards of the mammoth Clancy sagas. To Coonts this profit margin is ultimately a line of demarcation. On one side are war novelists the likes of Webb, James Jones, and Tim O'Brien. Their priorities have to do with realism and art. On the other are the new breed of genre writers who are mass-producing tehno-thrillers. The difference for Coonts is between what he calls "realistic, thoughtful novels" and "popular commercial fiction" which "makes absolutely no pretenses of being literature."

Publishers have been contracting writers by the score to pound out techno-thrillers. The result has been a glut of this kind of book in the nation's drug stores, airline terminals, newsstands, supermarkets and—oh yes!—book shops. The mass-market paperbacks are frequently emblazoned with glossy allusions to Clancy and Coonts in their cover copy.

This no doubt hastens the heartbeat of millions and does honor and justice to the genre. It also proves to the publicists in New York that you can always sell chicanery with its own gimcracks.

"I think that ultimately it's a fad," Coonts remarked. "A lot of the books are mediocre at best. I see a lot of shoot-'em-ups out there with high-tech stuff thrown in but not essential to the story. It's terrific that the guys who write them are breaking into publishing. Halleluia! But I think it'll pass. How many times can you do the next Korean War or the war in the Mideast? There's a limit on this stuff, and I think it's fast being reached. Tom Clancy can write anything he wants because he's a good-enough storyteller. He will always be able to sell his books. I'm a whole notch down from the public acceptance Tom Clancy's got. I'll have to grow and change to survive. But I guarantee you, I'm not about to do a book about the next Korean War or the war in the Mideast. I don't think the publishers are going to keep buying this stuff.". . .

GENERIC HEROES AND VILLAINS

One of the problems confronting writers in this genre is collaring a plausible villain. Cessation of the Cold War has all but eliminated the Red Army, the KGB, and other Russian golems. The Gulf War didn't last long enough to suit the television networks, let alone the quick-book publishers. "The terrorists are the only plausible villains around right now who are obvious," Coonts said. Tom Clancy rounded up terrorists, gangsters, and corrupt public officials foreign and domestic when he wrote his big one for 1989, *Clear and Present Danger* (Putnam). What we get is a pretty nifty book about the international drug war. Jack Ryan reappears as a three-star hero: CIA deputy director, concerned parent, and law-abiding citizen.

Jack Ryan would epitomize the "generic hero" if, as a character, he didn't raise such aggravating questions about himself. Annoying, because answers are never forthcoming. Reviewers and other readers often guess that he's the Walter Mitty projection of Tom Clancy.

Stephen Coonts presents another troublesome "generic" in the invention of Jake Grafton. Why should he warrant our attention? "Jake believes in himself," Coonts told me. "He is Everyman, with common sense and ability to do a good job. Jake Grafton is not wise, witty, or handsome. He is average. Jake is not a believer in high tech. Far from it. Jake has been in combat. He knows that, in real combat, anything more complex than a pocket watch won't work. Gadgets don't thrill Jake and don't thrill *me!* Jake is a timeless hero. I think that's Jake's appeal. He appeals to something basic in all of us."

But again, the hero of a brace of techno-thrillers has dimension because he has a job that he must do. This goes for all the techno-thrillers. The genre is about war, real, imagined, or inevitable. The job is warfare, the heroes are warriors. A case can be made that the authors in this genre are opting for a warrior class. Clancy denies that he's glorifying any such class but defers to the multivolume "Brotherhood of War" series. Those popular thrillers are the work of Coonts' friend Bill Butterworth, using the nom de plume W.E.B. Griffin.

TECHNO-THRILLER AS SUBGENRE OF SCIENCE FICTION

When he was a third-grade pupil, Tom Clancy began reading the fabulous novels of Jules Verne (1892–1905), the French author justly celebrated as the father of science fiction. Always an avid reader, Clancy has remained close to science fiction, for the pleasure of it and doubtless the inspiration in its otherworldly possibilities. While an English major at Baltimore's Loyola College, he completed an independent study program in science fiction. His reading list included Jules Verne, H.G. Wells, John Wyndham, Philip Wylie, and Isaac Asimov. He reached back to a literary genre that had captured his boyhood. It was clearly his intent to write science fiction stories. This he did, in some quantity, but was never fortunate to sell a single one to any publisher. Clancy told me that he never throws anything out. So, it's a safe bet that his SF manuscripts exist. Intuition tells me that they're probably well above average for contemporary SF tales. They would be the proving grounds for the techno-thriller. . . .

Clancy refers back to the eternal "What if . . ." of the science fiction visionaries. He applies their search for possibilities to modern warfare and foreign policy concerns. Among those classic prophetic writers, Jules Verne stands clearly apart as Tom Clancy's avatar.

In *The Hunt for Red October*, Clancy introduces Captain Marko Ramius, intrepid commander of the Soviet submarine *Red October*. Ramius is a man of parts. In early chapters the reader discovers his substance and ideals. Ramius proves to be more interesting than any other character in the story. His resemblance to an earlier seafaring warrior is unmistakable. *Twenty Thousand Leagues Under the Sea* (1870) is considered by many to be Jules Verne's finest work. Its central figure is Captain Nemo, master of the mysterious submarine *Nautilus*. When Verne wrote his novel, submarines only broke the waves in the minds of dreamers. What Clancy wrote about was a submarine so ingenious that the most sophisticated sonar devices could scarcely trace its undersea whisper. . . .

CLANCY'S LITERARY HERO

Jean Jules Verne, grandson of the great storyteller, relates how the author held vehement political convictions. He was incensed at the Russian oppression of the Polish people and others in Eastern Europe. Much of this acrimony found its way into an early draft of *Twenty Thousand Leagues Under the Sea*. Verne was prevailed upon by his business-wise publisher, Jules Hetzel, to purge any political material for the sake of high-volume international sales. Details of this restraint on the author are revealed in his grandson's *Jules Verne: A Biography*.

Nemo the obsessive-compulsive maverick is reincarnated as Ramius in *The Hunt for Red October*. He reappears as the Soviet defector in *The Cardinal of the Kremlin*, but only the mincing, incoherent shade of the pirate who stole away with the *Red October.* Tom Clancy summoned perhaps his only realized fictional character and set him adrift.

The authorship of Tom Clancy resembles Jules Verne's in an important way. Both men are telling prophetic stories dealing with quirks or innovations in scientific technology. In all important cases, knowledge of what is going on—or what is anticipated—is known to only a select cabal of men (and no women). Only in rare instances do any of these men ever impress us as well-conceived or realized personalities. This is all right with Clancy because his men are "generic." Jules Verne was criticized when the details of Nemo's *Nautilus* nearly put the character Nemo in total eclipse. Nonetheless, Verne taught Clancy, and Clancy taught "generics" to all the rest.

Those cells of privileged information aren't very interesting in Tom Clancy's books. Nearly always they are cadres of intelligence and secret weapons specialists who read Clausewitz in day school. Just drop a name like "Angleton" and you'll get a round of precise talk on the difference between *strategic* and *tactical.* Here are the Hollow Men. Heroes all.

PROJECTION OF PERSONALITY

Clancy told me that his favorite of his own novels is *Patriot Games*, the one he said was most "savaged" by reviewers. The story is outrageous and the characters are mostly clods. Technology is at a minimum. Instead we get bombs and an assortment of firearms, and the Clancy method of repelling international terrorists. The cabal is bestiary of Irish nationalist guerrillas led by Sean Miller, a convicted bomber. In another place, I have argued that Tom Clancy has such esteem for this work because it offered him an opportunity to pare his personality three ways. Accept Jack Ryan as Clancy's idealized self, no matter how loudly he denies it. His " generic" Prince of Wales appears callow, open-faced, a clean slate for the sage lessons of Jack Ryan. This Prince is an innocent with the power potential to be a warrior king. Perhaps another Clancy ideal. Sean Miller represents a special menace. When Jack Ryan testifies at the Old Bailey, he is chilled by Miller's cold stare. Clancy needed to create a duel, a shoot-out at Baltimore's Dundalk Marine Terminal, to do away with this ogre. I remain convinced that Sean Miller is Clancy's dark familiar, his *Doppelgänger*, the armed and dangerous one. Sean Miller is all that Clancy is not. Disorderly, unmilitary, reckless, anarchic. Clancy told me that he began to write *Patriot Games* well before he wrote *The Hunt for Red October*. By the luck of the Irish, the reading public came to know Tom Clancy far ahead of his prideful *Patriot Games*.

Curtis Church wrote a perceptive "Foreword" to the omnibus volume, *Works of Jules Verne* (1983). Therein, Church indicates Verne's schizoid outlook on modern science and its potentials. As much as he enjoyed science study and marveled at scientific advances, he dreaded the consequences of technology in mischievous or diabolical hands. Church further points to Verne's projection of his own personality in Captain Nemo and in Phileas Fogg, hero of *Around the World in Eighty Days* (1873; British, 1874). Thus the cabals, the secret enterprises of men who take dares and risk lives— their own or others. Jules Verne was a precise and thorough researcher. In his time he could never be faulted for inaccuracy. His personal insistence was on the plausible. The same is true of Tom Clancy today. He insisted to me that he has always relied on open, unclassified, or declassified source material, even though some of his novels have stunned and confounded people in Defense, as much of Verne was prophecy a century and more ago.

Playboy Interview: Tom Clancy

Marc Cooper

Critics commonly misconceive Tom Clancy as a writer with access to enough classified Pentagon secrets to warrant a terrorist attack. However, Marc Cooper found that Clancy relies on library research and an imagination bounded by realism—not friends in the CIA—to create the chilling and highly accurate descriptions of advanced weaponry that characterizes his novels. Tom Clancy admits that he never even set foot on board a submarine until after the publication of *The Hunt for Red October.*

In this 1988 interview, Clancy discusses his military vocabulary and familiarity with U.S.-Soviet relations in regard to nuclear weaponry. Clancy also gives insightful responses to questions pertaining to advanced military technology, his interest in technology as a human necessity, and his low opinion of the U.S. Congress.

Marc Cooper is a contributing editor to the *Nation* magazine, a columnist for *LA Weekly*, and a regular commentator for the *Los Angeles Times Sunday Opinion* section. His journalism has appeared in *Harpers,* the *New Yorker*, and *Rolling Stone.*

PLAYBOY: Through your best-selling novels, you've become a popular authority on what the U.S. and the Soviets really have in their military arsenals and on how war may be fought today. You've described American and Soviet military technology in such realistic detail that experts wonder how you do it. President Reagan is supposedly a big fan of yours. You *do* have sources at the CIA, don't you?

CLANCY: Not true. I've never had any official help from the intelligence community. Nor unofficial help.

PLAYBOY: How about help from the manufacturers of your favorite characters—submarines?

CLANCY: No, I never talked with anybody from General Dynamics. I didn't ever get aboard one of their submarines until after *The Hunt for Red October* was finished.

PLAYBOY: Where *did* you get your technical data?

CLANCY: [*Laughs*] From three books right here on my shelves: *Ships and Air Craft of the U.S. Fleet, Guide to the Soviet Navy, Combat Fleets of the World*, all from the Naval Institute Press. My current net investment is about $150. OK? And, you know, the Russians are asking the same questions as you are.

PLAYBOY: *Pravda* slammed you in a review titled "Caution: Poison" and warned that you were a mouthpiece for the Pentagon.

CLANCY: Yeah, but mainly, they wanted to know, "Who *is* that masked man?" They think I was elevated to my current affluence by the military-industrial complex; that General Dynamics needed an official minstrel, so they hired me instead of James Michener or something. There is no way a Russian could come to grips with the concept that I'm just a small businessman who reads a lot.

PLAYBOY: Maybe, maybe not. Our readers should know that this interview has already been interrupted by a call from a CIA agent.

CLANCY: That call? That was a guy whose department sponsored me when I gave a talk over at the CIA, that's all. I repeat: No one, but no one, has ever given me classified information of any kind. I've been told, however, that I *made up* material that turned out to be correct and very, very highly classified—but I don't know what it is. They tell me it's right but not what it is. Security spooks are very humorless people who have trouble believing that somebody can make a good guess. So do you guys in the media. Why can't you just give me credit for being smart?

PLAYBOY: We'll take your word for it, then. All your research is there on your shelf.

CLANCY: Yes. And for *The Hunt for Red October*, about nuclear subs, I also relied on a software war game called Harpoon. That's how I got my information on how weapons and ships and military lanes operate: how you maneuver a ship, how the radars work. There's a useful appendix in the manual; so it was easy. If you buy that game—and I guess it now costs $20 or so—you can spend maybe two hours a day with it for two weeks and you'll know as much about the Navy as some admirals.

PLAYBOY: That's a chilling thought.

CLANCY: And for *sure* you'll know more than anybody in Congress.

PLAYBOY: Shouldn't we be a little terrified that your fictional stories are being used as texts in our war colleges?

CLANCY: Not exactly as texts, but as case studies. What I do is paint in very broad strokes. I call it connect the dots: If you know this fact and that fact and that fact, you can figure out how they're connected. Evidently, I'm pretty good at that, or so a few generals and admirals tell me. . . .

PLAYBOY: And you believe that submarines *are* the crucial weapons of modern warfare. How do the subs—or boats, as you've taught us in your books to call them—of each country compare with each other?

CLANCY: American boats are quieter. They're mechanically far more reliable. Part of that comes from the fact that we have an overly conservative design philosophy. The Russians are willing to take a lot more design risks than we are. But because they have poor quality control, their good designs are poorly executed. And, therefore, they're mechanically unsafe, in many cases. . . .

PLAYBOY: Are American subs so much quieter and harder to detect than Soviet subs?

CLANCY: The amount of noise you make is a function of more than one thing. It's not just the speed or the power output of your reactor. It's also the configuration of the ship, because the ship itself makes noise as it goes through the water. And since the Soviets have more flooding holes in their hulls for the ballast tanks, their hulls are inherently noisier than ours.

PLAYBOY: This is what you have described as "hull-popping sounds"?

CLANCY: Right. It's more of a groan and a creak—a pop . . . snap, crackle and pop, like Rice Krispies. Ours don't do that as much, because we have fewer compartments. The bad news on our side is that their submarines are more survivable, because they're compartmented more closely and they can probably withstand more flooding than ours can. On the other hand, our design philosophy is that if they can't hear you, they ain't going to hit ya. Our props are quieter—or they *were* until some bastards in Japan and Norway gave the Russians the technology to duplicate them.

PLAYBOY: You're talking about the recent [1988] Toshiba scandal?

CLANCY: It wasn't just Toshiba; they had help. From Kongsberg, a Norwegian outfit that makes various technological devices and quite a few weapons systems.

PLAYBOY: And what is it, exactly, that Toshiba sold the Russians?

CLANCY: A computer-controlled milling machine that, with proper software, can be programmed to design this particular type of screw; they're very difficult to make. The Soviets had been trying to make them for some time; the ones they had were hand-lathed and not terribly well done. Now they'll be able to make them the same way we do. And I'm really pissed at those bastards!

PLAYBOY: Why so personal?

CLANCY: Toshiba helped make Russian submarines quieter. As a result of that, the lives of friends of mine who drive submarines for the U.S. Navy and the Royal Navy are very much more at risk now than they were before.

PLAYBOY: What do you think of the response from Congress?

CLANCY: What response? Congress is going to wimp out on this like they do on everything else. They see 4000 American jobs at risk if we come down hard on Toshiba. What about the 10,000 people we have out on submarines right now? What's more important, the job or somebody's life? . . .

PLAYBOY: It's not hard to guess your politics on this subject. Some of us think that Congress is too eager to support the Pentagon.

CLANCY: Oh, yeah? The day we went into Grenada, I think it was Jim Shannon, the former Congressman from Massachusetts who got on the floor of the House, for all the C-Span cameras, and recited, "Potato potahto, tomato, tomahto, Grenada, Grenahda, let's call the whole thing off." While that arrogant little bastard was saying that, real guns were firing real bullets at a friend of mine. A Navy helicopter pilot I knew was being shot at and he was awarded the Distinguished Flying Cross for saving 11 lives. He risked his life and some little prick of a Congressman was making jokes about it. That's wrong. That is just plain wrong.

PLAYBOY: You think Congress basically undermines the military?

CLANCY: What I'm saying is that it's Congress' job to help run the military, yet it doesn't keep up with what it's supposed to. When I spoke at the CIA last year, the talk was sponsored by the Office of Strategic Weapons Research. Over lunch, they had a good chuckle from saying that since *Red October* had been published, they'd had between 15 and 20 inquiries from Congress asking CIA how it was that the Soviets developed a submarine caterpillar drive before we did.

PLAYBOY: So?

CLANCY: So? So the caterpillar drive was totally fictional! I made it up out of whole cloth! Fifteen or 20 people on Capitol Hill could not tell the difference between a novel and an intelligence briefing. Don't you find that disturbing? Quite a few members of Congress lack either the time or the inclination to know what they're voting for. Decisions are made on an ideological rather than a factual basis. There's an old saying that the person who does not know how to ask the right question always hears the wrong answer. . . .

PLAYBOY: Some of what you say sounds right-wing and hard-line; but some doesn't. What do you call yourself?

CLANCY: People call me a hawk. Actually, I find myself to be fairly reasonable, pragmatic. The political right consistently overestimates the threat of the Soviet Union to the United States. There is a real threat, it is a threat that we should be very concerned about, but if you distort the threat, if you overestimate the nature of your enemy, if you say he's a lot more formidable than he really is, all you're doing is robbing credibility from the threat that actually exists, and that's just stupid. . . .

PLAYBOY: So, again, you see the problem as political.

CLANCY: Yes. Political leadership says, "We have a job for you; here it is, go do it." And the military salutes, says "Yes, sir" and goes off and does its best. In the case of Vietnam, the Army was sent to do something for which it had no clear mission description. President Johnson said, "It is necessary for the United States to go fight in Vietnam." The military said "Yes, sir" and put its plans and recommendations together and went back to President Johnson and he read them over and said, "No, you can't do it that way. You have to do it this way. It's politically necessary." And the military did its best and it failed. . . .

PLAYBOY: Let's play one of your war scenarios: What could actually trigger an East-West conflict in Europe?

CLANCY: A likely one these days? OK. As in *Red Storm Rising*, Moslem dissidents in the Soviet Union—and they have a lot of Moslems—sabotage the major domestic Soviet oil fields. Faced with a crippling energy crunch, and lacking hard-currency reserves to import the oil, the Soviets are forced to seize the Middle Eastern oil fields. To clear the way for such an adventure, they must first take out the Western military alliance, NATO.

PLAYBOY: So the Soviets begin a land war in Europe.

CLANCY: Precisely. They launch a massive surprise attack against West Germany and try to overwhelm us with sheer force of numbers and armor. Those are their strong points: size and proximity.

PLAYBOY: What would the West do in the first days?

CLANCY: Throw everything we've got against them to prevent a breakthrough in our lines. Concentrate as many troops as possible on the front. And now comes the tricky part: Resupplying our troops in Europe means sending convoys of freighters across 3000 miles of the Atlantic Ocean.

PLAYBOY: The Russians are going to try to sink those ships.

CLANCY: That's why they have 300 fast-attack subs! Their ability to choke off our resupply hinges on getting enough submarines away from their coast and into the middle of the Atlantic to attack our convoys.

PLAYBOY: So from a planned Soviet attack on the Middle East, fighting first moves to the land in Europe and ultimately to a battle for the Atlantic.

CLANCY: Yes, because if we're able to freely resupply our troops in Europe, we can probably win the war. If not, we can lose.

PLAYBOY: How does the U.S. keep the Atlantic free from Soviet attack forces?

CLANCY: OK, you have to picture the Soviet fleet concentrated up in the northern corner of Europe. The Soviets have to take their fleet down into the main Atlantic through a relatively narrow corridor. On the northern border of that passage is Greenland. On the southern extreme is England. In the middle of this channel is Iceland.

PLAYBOY: And NATO's goal would be to block that passage.

CLANCY: Right. That's why we have what is called the

Greenland-Iceland-U.K. line, G./I./U.K. It's like a fence across the northern Atlantic.

PLAYBOY: And that's why you ascribe such importance to the island nation of Iceland.

CLANCY: What most people don't understand is that Iceland is the key to Europe. If we hold Iceland, the Russian job of closing the North Atlantic goes from difficult to damn near impossible. That's why, in *Red Storm Rising*, we let the Soviets neutralize Iceland.

PLAYBOY: We let them?

CLANCY: Well, I let them. I came up with a very good plan for them, didn't I? Some papers have been written about it at the Naval War College, as a matter of fact.

PLAYBOY: How heavily does NATO patrol that fence?

CLANCY: We keep a pretty close eye on their subs at all times. In a war, we would essentially set up a toll-booth operation and try to clobber each sub as it tried to squeeze through. It would cost them a lot to get their submarines out.

PLAYBOY: There is also a sort of electronic barrier along this fence, isn't there?

CLANCY: Yes. The SOSUS line—that's an acronym for Sound Surveillance System. Hydrophones. Underwater listening devices deployed all over the area. There's a line from Greenland to Iceland to the U.K. And probably a number of similar lines up in the Barents Sea, north of the Soviet Union. And I daresay the Norwegian Sea is also wired like a pinball machine. . . .

CLANCY: In a chapter in *Red Storm Rising*, I proposed one way: The Russians do something smart. They use half their attack force to launch decoys, and we go for the decoys while the actual strike force comes in from a different direction. Any army—or navy—can be done in by a stupid commander. As I said earlier, usually, the side with brains is the side that wins.

PLAYBOY: But in our scenario, the one you think is most

likely today, if the Soviets were to attack in Europe but failed to take Iceland—

CLANCY: Then we'd run the ships across the Atlantic and resupply our troops in Europe. And we'd probably win.

PLAYBOY: Wait. The U.S. has all those Soviet submarines bottled up in their sanctuaries. Do we just go in and kill their subs?

CLANCY: You said it! You think that's unsporting?

PLAYBOY: No, just dangerous.

CLANCY: Hey, that's their job, to kill everything they find. That's how you get promoted—in peacetime, you get promoted by pushing paper better than anybody else. In wartime, you get promoted for killing people. It's called sanitizing the area.

PLAYBOY: There you are, off the Soviet coast, destroying all their nuclear subs. You really don't think the Russians just might consider the nuclear option at that point?

CLANCY: No. The Russians are more realistic on nuclear issues than we are. They know that if they have ships out there, some of them are going to get lost.

PLAYBOY: OK. We win in that scenario. Since most war scenarios begin with a Soviet land invasion of Europe, just how likely is an invasion to happen in real life?

CLANCY: Not very. In *Red Storm Rising*, I was very careful to *force* the decision upon the Soviets. I don't think they have any particular intention to go off and conquer the world— overtly.

PLAYBOY: You don't agree with those who say communism is inherently expansionist?

CLANCY: Their political beliefs militate against that, not in favor of it. The Soviets believe, and Marxism-Leninism teaches them, that sooner or later, the whole world is going to go Communist, because communism is the ultimate expression of human society. They really believe that, in the same sense that a born-again Christian believes in the *Epistles* of Saint Paul. Consequently, if everything you believe tells you that you're ultimately going to win—why risk everything on one throw of the dice? It simply is not a logical thing to do.

PLAYBOY: Are you a supporter of the treaty Gorbachev and Reagan signed banning intermediate missiles?

CLANCY: I thought it was a good agreement for everybody. Good for them, good for us, good for the whole world.

PLAYBOY: Why?

CLANCY: Because you're eliminating weapons that in my view simply were not militarily useful. They were more dangerous than useful. And therefore, the world's a safer place without them.

PLAYBOY: Yet in *Red Storm*, you have a slick Russian leader who fools the U.S. with arms-reduction proposals, only to mask his intent to invade. Is he supposed to sound like Gorbachev?

CLANCY: No, not at all. That scenario was put together before Gorbachev was elevated at the Politburo. The fact that my premier came out of a background of agriculture, as did Gorbachev, is another one of those coincidences. . . .

PLAYBOY: In all of your books, but most notably in *Patriot Games*, there is constant reference to good guys and bad guys. Is the world really that simple?

CLANCY: A lot of the good-guy, bad-guy stuff in *Patriot Games* is a technical designation. That's the way cops talk. It is, nevertheless, the way I think in a lot of cases. The world is not so simple as to lend itself to people's falling into one of two categories. But those two categories do exist and quite a few people do fall into them.

PLAYBOY: Do you reject the notion of other writers, such as John Le Carré, that there might exist some moral symmetry between "our side" and "theirs"? That, ultimately, we're all up to the same thing?

CLANCY: That's an absurd notion. Today, in Afghanistan, the Russians are deploying a munition, a bomb, that's completely new, unique in the history of warfare. It is an antichild bomb. Dan Rather showed a clip of it on TV. It has to be real. It's a bomb that's in the configuration of a toy—a truck or a doll. A kid picks it up and it blows his hand off. There is no moral symmetry between the United States and the Soviet Union. Certainly, we've never deployed anything like that. In our darkest hour—and some of the things we did in Vietnam we don't have to be especially proud of—we never have done anything like that.

PLAYBOY: Some would say that your faith in the good guys is wishful thinking. Like your faith in technology.

CLANCY: Let me ask you a question. In what kind of airplane did you fly from Los Angeles to Washington to interview me?

PLAYBOY: A 747.

CLANCY: Did you feel safe?

PLAYBOY: Most of the time. Not as much as some years ago.

CLANCY: Well, the 747 is a pretty good bird. The only times they ever broke have been the crew's fault. If it weren't for technology—let's say, for example, if you took away fertilizers, which are chemically manufactured, and just eliminated them worldwide—50 percent of the people alive today would be dead in 12 months.

That's what technology does for us. It keeps us alive. I'm driving a car with German engineering. You're using a Sony tape recorder, Japanese engineering. You couldn't make a living without it. We get our information that way. Business could barely function today without computers. Technology is part of life, and always has been. Ever since we stopped using our muscles to poke holes in the ground to plant seeds, technology has been important. After it's been around for 20 years or so, it just recedes into the woodwork. There was a time when nails were high-tech.

PLAYBOY: When did your great romance with technology begin?

CLANCY: I've always been a gadget freak. When I was back in first grade, I think it was the first year that the Walt Disney show was on TV. There was a one-hour show of how the space race was going to start. I saw that and I said, "Yeah, that's the way to go." And I've been a technology freak ever since. I supported the space program before there even was one! That's where the future is. The future is in doing things that we don't know how to do yet.

PLAYBOY: Don't you think an increasingly technological society undermines the human side of life?

CLANCY: Why should it? I have two computers and a couple of VCRs, color TVs and all that neat stuff. I still like to talk with my family over dinner. Maybe they said the same thing when Gutenberg perfected the movable-type press. The real synonym for technology is tool. Any item of technology is simply a tool. If it's used skillfully, it has a positive effect on the way life is lived. If it's used unskillfully, or stupidly, as often happens, it can kill people.

PLAYBOY: Yet a lot of people have begun asking questions about the role of technology—its impact on the environment, on who controls the technology and, most recently, about whether or not complex technology even works the way it's supposed to. Do you have any second thoughts such as those?

CLANCY: Absolutely not. Most of the people who say that are living off in never-never land. In past centuries, such people were called Luddites. Technology is part of life. It's not going to go away. As far as its working, well, people are people, and they will continue to make mistakes, to screw up.

PLAYBOY: But doesn't technology sometimes amplify those mistakes? Screwing up with a nail is one thing; with a nuclear power plant, it's quite another.

CLANCY: Technology makes things *safer*. Let's take Three Mile Island, for example. The people screwed up real bad. The technology built into the power plant saved them. There was enough safety built into the system itself to prevent anything really bad from happening. And, in fact, nothing really bad happened. Nobody was hurt. There may be one extra case of cancer 20 years from now; and if there is, it'll probably be a jerk like me who smokes.

PLAYBOY: You wouldn't have any problem living next to a nuclear power plant?

CLANCY: I *do* live next to one—15 miles from a nuclear power plant. The place we just bought on Chesapeake Bay is in a direct line of sight to it. Doesn't concern me.

PLAYBOY: What about the Soviet disaster at Chernobyl? Do you think it was a technological breakdown or just human error?

CLANCY: It was probably both. Name one Soviet consumer product, aside from the AK-47 assault rifle, which was, in fact, stolen from the Germans; it was originally the German StG 44—that you can buy in the West. Cars? Television sets? Cameras? Maybe caviar—but the fish make that. Soviet technology is not terribly impressive. I've been inside Soviet military equipment. I'm not overwhelmed.

PLAYBOY: Why do you think it's so inferior?

CLANCY: Politics. Their economy is screwed up. In America, either you turn out a quality product or nobody buys it. And if nobody buys it, you go broke. In the Soviet Union, they don't have market forces to regulate anything. If a guy turns out a quality product and he's the only one who makes it, the people have to buy it whether it's good or not. You can make an argument that the best reflection of any society is to be found in its military, because all of its societal tendencies and all of its economic abilities will be crystallized at that level. Every time American gear has met Soviet gear on the battlefield, the Soviets have come off second best.

PLAYBOY: Back to the future. Your next book is *Cardinal of the Kremlin*, and we understand that it focuses on Star Wars—

CLANCY: Don't call it that. Come on.

PLAYBOY: Why not?

CLANCY: It's a pejorative name for something that can be of great benefit to the world. The Strategic Defense Initiative, SDI.

PLAYBOY: Why are you such an ardent booster of such a controversial program?

CLANCY: It offers us the only logical way out that I see of the nuclear conundrum that we're in now. Nuclear deterrence, the situation that putatively keeps the peace in the world today, is fundamentally flawed. It's like a bunch of crazed neighbors with loaded shotguns marching around their homes, yelling death threats at one another. Just because it happens to be nation-states that agree to keep the peace that way doesn't make it any less crazy.

PLAYBOY: Instead of coming up with new gadgets that may not work, why not try to take the shotguns away—in this case, the nuclear weapons?

CLANCY: You're *never* going to eliminate all nuclear weapons. You're *never* going to eliminate manned bombers. You're *never* going to eliminate cruise missiles.

PLAYBOY: Why not?

CLANCY: Because there simply is no way to verify their elimination. You want to bring a nuclear bomb into the U.S.? Don't bring it in on a missile. Just disguise it as cocaine and bring it through the Miami airport. [*Laughs*] However, we might be able to get rid of the *scary* missiles, the long-range ballistic weapons.

PLAYBOY: So how would Star Wars, or SDI, do that? . . .

CLANCY: You take a free-electron laser and base it on the ground.

PLAYBOY: Not in space?

CLANCY: Oh, no! You want the laser on the ground, so you can fix it when it breaks. That way, you don't have any trouble getting power to it. This laser shoots up a single beam of light with a power on the order of 10,000,000 watts. That searing beam hits a mirror that is up in orbit. That mirror relays the beam to a second mirror, which then focuses the beam and aims it down at a Soviet rocket just as it is emerging from its ground silo. . . .

PLAYBOY: You obviously love this military stuff, yet you

were kept out of the Service because of poor eyesight. Do you think you'd rather be doing it for real, instead of just writing about it?

CLANCY: I've told all my friends in the military that I'd rather do what *they* do than what *I* do. The reason is, I'm just a minstrel, when you get down to it. OK, I may be a very smart minstrel, or a very lucky minstrel, or a very successful minstrel. But I'm just a minstrel. And people out there who do this work every day are more important than I am, and they do not get the recognition that I do.

PLAYBOY: Is there a message you're trying to get through in your novels?

CLANCY: My feeling on messages comes from Sam Gold-wyn: If you want to send a message, use Western Union. But if there *is* a message in what I write, it is that the people who serve in the U.S. military are in essentially the same kind of work as police officers and firemen. Their job is to risk their lives for people they don't know. I don't say they're perfect, and they don't claim to be perfect; but they are entitled to as much respect.

PLAYBOY: When did you decide you were going to be a writer?

CLANCY: It was always my dream. I wanted to see my name on the cover of a book.

PLAYBOY: But you didn't publish anything until you were an adult. And then it was a letter to the editor.

CLANCY: Yeah. To the *Proceedings of the U.S. Naval Institute*, the monthly journal of the U.S. Naval Institute. I said that it wasn't doing its job properly of explaining its role to the American people—that the United States needs a Navy. What the Navy people were mainly doing was communicating back and forth among themselves. Totally incestuous.

PLAYBOY: Turns out that you've taken over that job for yourself.

CLANCY: Never thought of it that way. Yeah.

PLAYBOY: Was it your Jesuit education that instilled in you

the discipline to sit in front of a word processor eight hours a day?

CLANCY: Do I look like a very disciplined person? [*Waves at the cluttered study around him*] I tend to be something of a slob. I fight against it, but it seems to be a losing battle. I tend to be lazy. Though my writing is the first disciplined thing that I've been able to do in my life. It took me 35 years, but I've finally found something I'm good at. I guess it just took me a long time to grow up.

CHAPTER 2

Reviews and Analyses of Tom Clancy's Major Works

READINGS ON
TOM CLANCY

Clancy's Accuracy Makes
The Hunt for Red October Successful

Kirk H. Beetz

Kirk H. Beetz asserts that in *The Hunt For Red October,* Tom Clancy encapsulates his perception of Soviet and American cultural differences, and that these differences are what motivate Clancy's characters. Beetz goes on to identify this contrast between American and Soviet society as a major theme of Clancy's novel. Other themes Beetz identifies are betrayal and technology.

Beetz also remarks that although most of Clancy's characters are stereotypes, some, such as *Red October*'s commander, Marko Ramius, are more completely developed. Beetz concludes by suggesting that Clancy's knack of creating strong, easily identifiable characters helps hold the reader's interest.

Kirk H. Beetz is the coeditor of Beacham's Popular Fiction. He has also written biographies of C.S. Lewis, Cynthia Voight, and Tennessee Williams.

The plot of *The Hunt for Red October* may focus on the attempt of a Soviet submarine captain and his officers to defect to the United States, but the reaons for the defection are social, not military. The motivations of characters and their interactions with each other are founded in Clancy's perceptions of Soviet and American societies. Marko Ramius, captain of the Russian submarine *Red October*, is a carefully drawn character. He is Lithuanian and the son of a powerful Communist Party leader. Much of his rise to his role as the Soviet Union's

Kirk H. Beetz, "Thomas L. Clancy Jr., 1947," *Beacham's Popular Fiction in America,* edited by Walter Beacham. Washington, DC: Beacham, 1986. Copyright © 1986 by Beacham Publishing. Reproduced by permission.

premier expert on submarine warfare has been based on his father's influence. Far from being grateful to his father and the Party, Ramius is troubled and angry. He is tormented by the memory of the time he told his father of the dissenting views of a schoolmate's father and of how that unfortunate man subsequently disappeared forever. His classmates shunned him as a snitch; as he grew up, he was denied comfort in the Roman Catholic church because the Communist Party brutally suppressed religious practices. To Ramius, his father was responsible for the suppression of Lithuanian culture, and he felt that he shared his father's guilt.

RUSSIAN AND AMERICAN SOCIETIES

The Soviet Union is portrayed as an unhappy society in which variety of opinion and culture is impermissible. "Marxism-Leninism was a jealous god," writes Clancy, "tolerating no competing loyalties." Competence is usually determined by party loyalty, not proficiency in one's job. As a consequence, a drunken surgeon butchers Ramius' beloved wife and yet is protected from punishment by bureaucrats in the Communist Party. Ramius is very good at designing and running submarines; his skill is threatening to Party functionaries. When he takes the new supersubmarine *Red October* out for a trial shakedown voyage, he knows it may be his last trip because Party officials may not give him another command; this knowledge, his bitterness over his wife's death, and his guilt from his childhood inspire him to plot to turn over the *Red October*, replete with nuclear ballistic missiles, to the United States.

America, in contrast, is a cocky society whose military men are proud of the country and their military hardware. Ramius had chosen a naval career to escape from the day-to-day strictures of his society; Americans such as Bart Mancuso, captain of the attack submarine *Dallas*, chose naval careers not only for adventure, but to serve their country by defending it. Even C.I.A. agents, often portrayed in American fiction of the 1970s and 1980s as connivers who subvert the law for their own ends, are shown to be good people who battle to keep foreign enemies from harming the United States.

America's open society produces independent thinkers; although their freedom to think for themselves can be advantageous, a few American servicemen come dangerously close to disobeying orders and possibly starting a war. Russia's closed society produces obedient people whose adherence to rules inhibits their ability to respond to surprises; nonetheless, the Russian commitment to duty makes them relentless and dangerous foes. Clancy's views of the relative merits of each society are made clear by his focusing on Marko Ramius, a man tormented by his society. If the novel is to have a moral victory, then the Soviet Union must lose, because it crushes the spirits of even its best men.

THEMES: BETRAYAL AND TECHNOLOGY

The contrast between Soviet and American societies as exemplified by their militaries is a major theme of *The Hunt for Red October*, but it is not the only one. Another significant theme that is played out on several levels of the novel is that of betrayal. When the story begins, Marko Ramius has already completed his plans to betray his government. He is motivated by his hatred for the communist system, by disgust at its treatment of his countrymen, the Lithuanians, and by a desire to punish the Soviet government. A tightly self-controlled man, he does not lash out at those who have hurt him but instead determines how best to harm his government and then schemes for months to put his fellow conspirators in the right places for success. Ramius' betrayal is a calculated response to a cruel and stifling society. It is a gesture of independence.

Betrayals can take several forms. Some can be coolly calculated, like that of Ramius. Others can be routine, like the reports of naval "political officers" who reveal to the Communist Party the deviations from doctrine of their shipmates. Others can be the products of foolishness, as in the case of Peter Henderson, aide to a powerful United States Senator who has often given the C.I.A. trouble. Dismayed by the shooting of student protestors at Kent State and the bombing of Cambodia during the Vietnam War, Henderson gave Soviet K.G.B. agents some information. As a C.I.A. agent put it, the K.G.B. "offers the hook, and he nibbled at it. A few years later, of course, they stuck the hook nice and hard and he couldn't get away." Henderson's treason betrayed American foreign agents, resulting in their deaths; the C.I.A. not only traps him but uses his betrayal to force the Senator into retirement.

Betrayals and deceptions throughout *The Hunt for Red October* create suspense because almost anyone could be a spy—even a ship's cook—and because no one can be sure others are telling the truth. For instance, even as he announces his betrayal, Ramius lies by declaring that he is sailing for New York City, although he intends to sail for another port. Lies within lies and betrayals within betrayals give the novel a consistent air of suspenseful uncertainty until its climax.

Another important theme is that of advanced technology. The social theme provides motivations for characters. The theme of betrayal reveals how the characters go about their business. The theme of technology reveals what the characters can and cannot do; advanced technology at once enables characters to pursue their goals and limits their options. Nearly everyone in *The Hunt for Red October* is dependent on technology. Ramius counts on his submarine's new quiet propulsion system to enable him to evade pursuers; the Americans count on their listening devices to pick up the sound of *Red October* so that they may find it before its pursuers do.

Technology unites the other themes. For instance, it is a product of different social systems. The Soviets emphasize duty and commitment to the principles of Marxism-

Leninism. Therefore their military demands absolute obedience by enlisted men to their officers. Their submarines are designed to limit the access crewmen have to sophisticated equipment. For instance, only officers may use sonar equipment. Furthermore, crewmen are exposed to dangerous equipment because individual people are not as important as are the goals of their government. American and British ships, in contrast, seem almost luxurious. Comfortable quarters, good food, and safe equipment are important on U.S. ships. The Soviet sailors make wry jokes about the "softness" of their Western counterparts; the Americans view the designs of Russian nuclear submarines as primitive and too dangerous.

Technology repeatedly betrays the Soviets. Americans have a significant advantage over their counterparts and sometimes surprise the Soviets by being able to anticipate Soviet moves by tracking ships and aircraft with equipment much more sophisticated than that of the Soviets. Even Ramius is surprised to learn that his submarine's quiet propulsion system has been heard and tracked by American technicians. The Soviets push their sailors and equipment hard. Eventually one attack submarine is pushed too hard as it sacrifices safety for speed, and its nuclear reactor has a catastrophic core melt-down, sending the craft to the bottom of the ocean, trapping the sailors in an immobile tomb.

RAMIUS, RYAN, AND MANCUSO

The Hunt for Red October has many characters, most of whom are well-sketched stereotypes, such as self-assured National Guard pilots eager to prove themselves the equals of regular servicemen and political officers declaiming Communist Party platitudes. However, a few characters are fleshed out with personalities all their own. The most interesting of these is Marko Ramius, the brilliant and intense commander of *Red October*. Without him there would be no story; therefore, it is important that he and his motivations be thoroughly developed.

Ramius is a product of Soviet society, even though he detests it. His life has made him ruthless in furthering his own ends. For example, he kills *Red October*'s political officer with his bare hands and gives little indication that the cold-blooded murder troubles his conscience. In order to survive in his society, Ramius has learned to hide his emotions, and he seems to eventually deny those emotions, such as compassion, that would be taken as signs of weakness and lack of Marxist-Leninist resolve. His efforts to hide his true feelings from his father and other Party functionaries seem to have made him cautious. Therefore, when he resolves to defect with *Red October*, his lifetime of experience in surviving in a cutthroat society makes him both capable of elaborate yet secretive planning, and ruthless enough to do whatever is necessary for success. On the other hand, he is not a psychopath; instead, he is a thoughtful man whose great suffering humanizes him. He desperately wants to be a better man. His battle against the forces of a society that has made his life miserable makes him a sympathetic character. Not wholly good nor wholly bad, Ramius is a well-rounded character.

Two other characters are also notable. One is Jack Ryan, the humane C.I.A. agent, and the other is Bart Mancuso, the vigorous captain of America's attack submarine *Dallas*. Ryan is fun to follow because he defies literary conventions. Instead of being a killing machine, he is a scholar; instead of being an outgoing lady's man, he is shy and a settled family man. Far from fearless, he is nervous about flying and uncomfortable in his undercover roles. He expresses the emotions that ordinary people would likely feel in similar circumstances, making him a character that most readers can identify with.

Mancuso, on the other hand, is more stereotyped. He is young because the United States Navy only puts young officers in charge of nuclear submarines. Like his Russian counterparts, he is devoted to duty. Unlike them, he is devoted to his duty as he understands it, not as it has been dictated to him by a "political officer," and he feels free to express doubts about the wisdom of orders he is expected to follow. In a way, he is the reflection of the American frontier hero; he is brash, aggressive, confident, manly, boyishly charming, and clean cut. Some readers are disturbed by the characterization of Mancuso and other American servicemen, finding them menacing in their reluctance sometimes to follow standing orders. However, there is a touch of realism to Mancuso and his fellows, and their stereotypical daring and courage make them powerfully appealing to Americans who still admire the frontier spirit.

CLANCY'S TECHNIQUES FOR CHARACTERIZATION

Clancy is a first-rate storyteller. He creates interesting characters, involves them in interesting events, and fills his plot with surprises and inventive challenges. In writing *The Hunt for Red October*, Clancy had two major difficulties to overcome. The first was the large number of characters and settings that his tale required; readers can quickly lose interest if they cannot keep track of the characters. The other difficulty was how to present all the technological information without bogging down the plot in technical details.

He solves the first problem by first sketching characters with bold images. The novel begins with its strongest character, Marko Ramius. By the end of the first page, Ramius is shown to be a "Captain First Rank" in the Soviet Navy who is a keen observer of his Arctic surroundings. By the end of "The First Day," Ramius has been given a bold outline: He is thoughtful and strong-willed and has a tragic past. Jack Ryan is similarly highlighted when first introduced. In less than a page, he is shown to be a scholarly family man and an unlikely hero. Not only are characters presented in sharp images, but they are given interesting problems to overcome. Thus readers can become interested in the exploits of several characters because each is clearly defined and active in the events of the novel.

The realistic portrayals of characters help humanize the technology. They are the focus of the story, and technology is not presented in long paragraphs of detailed explanation, a danger in a plot that is dependent on technology for its exciting situations. The technical information is blended in with the actions of the characters. For instance, the capabilities of the sonar for the U.S.S. *Dallas* are revealed through the reactions of Sonarman Second Class Ronald Jones, who on hearing the strange propulsion system of *Red October* for the first time says, "It's not screw sounds, not whales or fish. More likely water going through a pipe." In just a couple of lines, Clancy reveals that the sonar is so acute that it can even identify fish, and at the same time the plot is moved forward because Jones has heard the elusive *Red October*, and the Americans can now join the chase.

Red Storm Rising Is a Well-Told Story

Robert Lekachman

Robert Lekachman reviews *Red Storm Rising* and points out the fact that the novel is successful because not only does Tom Clancy know how to appeal to the American public's interest in state-of-the-art weaponry and technology, but because the courage and honor displayed by his characters make them attractive to readers.

Lekachman does not contend that Clancy is a particularly talented or complex writer, noting that his characters are rather predictable, but the plots are always action-packed and compelling, and there is a certain comfort in the knowledge that America will prevail.

Robert Lekachman taught economics at Lehman College in Bronx, New York. His book *Visions and Nightmares: America After Reagan* was published in 1987.

Tom Clancy's first novel, the best-selling "Hunt for Red October," was a superior example of the technological thriller, a genre that awards equal billing to human actors and state-of-the-art computers, missiles, devices of detection and deception, spy satellites, nuclear submarines and Mach 2 or Mach 3 fighter planes. Men, and even an occasional woman, prevail when they outwit their opponents with better deployment of exotic tools, not necessarily superior in design to those in the enemy arsenal. Skilled spinners of such *au courant* [fully informed] tales, among them Mr. Clancy, appeal simultaneously to the universal appetite for individual heroics and the special American affection for high tech.

Robert Lekachman, "Virtuous Men and Perfect Weapons," *The New York Times Book Review*, July 27, 1986, pp. 7–8. Copyright © 1986 by The New York Times Company. Reproduced by permission.

PLOT IN *RED STORM RISING*

"The Hunt for Red October" focused on the attempted defection of a single Soviet submarine. Success has increased Mr. Clancy's ambition. His new theme is nothing less than World War III. The conflict begins in western Siberia one starry night when a band of Moslem extremists ignite a huge oil refinery complex and eliminate a third of the Soviet Union's crude oil production for as many as three years. How is the Politburo to cope with this?

The answer is in the Persian Gulf. No serious military obstacle bars Soviet troops from cheap, abundant Saudi oil. It's there for the seizing. Trouble is, NATO would surely make armed reprisals against the Soviet Union at the hint of a Middle Eastern incuration. To the majority of the Politburo, the situation's logic is inexorable: NATO must be defeated before action in the Persian Gulf. In the hope of splitting NATO politically, the K.G.B. directs a massive disinformation operation, the centerpiece of which is a bomb plot supposedly designed by the West Germans to assassinate the entire Politburo. To lend the scheme credibility, a bomb actually kills a group of Russian children about to receive an award in Moscow. If the deception succeeds, NATO will disintegrate, leaving the West Germans unprotected and the route to oil open.

But NATO holds firm. The Politburo gambles and sends Soviet troops to invade Western Europe. The remainder of the novel deals with the ebb and flow of battle as seen on the American side by such representative figures as a nuclear submarine commander, the captain of a frigate, a gruff naval aviator and a young Navy meteorologist, code-named Beagle, who becomes a vital intelligence source in Soviet-occupied Iceland. The narrative cuts back and forth among military action in West Germany, the war at sea and in the air and Beagle's fortunes. For good measure, Mr. Clancy briefs us from time to time on Kremlin political deliberations and developments.

Although the writing is unduly *prolix* [prolonged or

drawn out], especially in its loving treatment of submarine warfare, the story is well told. The many readers of Mr. Clancy's first book will enjoy "Red Storm Rising." His is an oddly comforting version of World War III. Neither nuclear nor chemical weapons are employed by either side, although the Kremlin hard-liners come perilously close to resorting to them when the tide of battle in West Germany and at sea begins to turn against the Soviet forces. But not even conventional bombers are unleashed against civilians. Just as in World War I, almost all the victims are in uniform.

There is particularly good news here for Defense Secretary Caspar Weinberger. With exceedingly minor exceptions, American technology works—spy satellites, Stealth aircraft, advanced tanks and sonar, the lot. The excellence of our weapons and the bravery of our fighting men—and of a certain fighting woman, Maj. Army Nakamura of the Air Force—blunt the Soviet advance through West Germany. After dreadful losses, American convoys make it to European ports with vital men, weapons and equipment. Our wily commander in Europe takes a walk in the woods with his Soviet counterpart, and they talk sense. A thoroughly good type, the Soviet commander presides over a Kremlin coup that offers a vague project of more enlightenment at home and abroad.

MORAL HEROES

Mr. Clancy's undistinguished prose is serviceable enough not to impede the flow of his narrative. His characterizations are on a Victorian boys' book level. All the Americans are paragons of courage, endurance and devotion to service and country. Their officers are uniformly competent and occasionally inspired. Men of all ranks are faithful husbands and devoted fathers. As when knighthood was in flower, the enemy is almost equally virtuous. Russian submarine commanders and generals are skilled in the lethal arts. Enlisted personnel fight as valiantly as the Americans and West Germans. The bad Russians are the Politburo Stalinists and the K.G.B. political officers who shadow and sabotage military commanders.

Don't get me wrong. Occasional *longueurs* [dull and tedious passages] aside, I enjoyed this rattling good yarn for the same reasons I used to curl up with one of C.S. Forester's Horatio Hornblower adventures. Lots of action. Good men in tight spots. The comforting certainty that our side will win. Mr. Clancy has left the world in sufficiently tidy shape so that, if he is so inclined, he can favour us someday with the story of World War IV.

The Cardinal of the Kremlin Is a Great Spy Novel

Bob Woodward

In this favorable review of *The Cardinal of the Kremlin*, Bob Woodward praises Clancy's portrayal of his Soviet characters. Woodward asserts that despite the fact that Tom Clancy's public persona is unapologetically superpatriotic, *The Cardinal of the Kremlin* demonstrates a sympathy for the Soviet Union that comes through in the depth and sophistication of his Soviet characters.

Woodward also commends Clancy for using his popularity to bolster public awareness of the flaws in relying on the strategy of Mutual Assured Destruction, which at the time of this viewpoint's publication was the basis of both superpowers' nuclear policy.

Bob Woodward was an assistant managing editor of the *Washington Post* and the author of *Veil: The Secret Wars of the CIA, 1981–1987*.

Tom Clancy has written a great spy novel. I count several reasons why *The Cardinal of the Kremlin* rivals Clancy's *The Hunt for Red October*, surpasses his *Red Storm Rising* and runs circles around his *Patriot Games*.

The new novel has the authentic feel of espionage, at once the most coy and the most deadly of statecraft arts. The story moves on at least 10 action fronts, and Clancy shifts gracefully among them. They include a CIA-supported unit of Afghan freedom fighters; the CIA's senior officials—among them Clancy's hero from previous novels, Jack Ryan; the CIA's Moscow station; the Oval Office in the White House;

Bob Woodward, "The Hunt for the Red Mole," *The Washington Post*, July 3, 1988. Copyright © 1988 by The Washington Post Writers Group. Reproduced by permission.

the crew of the attack submarine U.S.S. Dallas (from *Hunt for Red October*); arms-control negotiators in Moscow; the secret U.S. test site for "Star Wars" weapons (President Reagan's Strategic Defense Initiative); the secret Russian test site for similar weapons; the Soviet Defense Ministry; and the central offices of the KGB, the Communist Party and the Politburo. An American mole has burrowed himself near the heart of the Kremlin, and the race is on for the CIA to get out one final report from their agent before the KGB puts him out of business. All this against the very real backdrop of the U.S.-Soviet competition to be first with a deployable anti-ballistic missile (or Star Wars) system. Indeed, *The Cardinal of the Kremlin* could have been titled "The Hunt for the Red Mole."

It offers a marvelous portrait of the Soviet Union and Moscow. The U.S.S.R. scenes are as good as anything in Martin Cruz Smith's very popular 1981 novel, *Gorky Park*. Clancy delivers with the nitty-gritty detail of spy work in the field: document transfers, brush contacts, chalk marks, surveillance, counter-surveillance and the like. Clearly some spooks have spilled the secrets of tradecraft to him. In particular, there is an excellent study of counterintelligence work. The KGB's Colonel Vatutin must find the mole, and some painstaking policework follows. At his disposal are the most chilling "modern" interrogation techniques. The colonel is plagued, by the way, with the eternal Moscow (and Washington) question: Does the front office want to know the full truth?

The energy for the conflict comes from Clancy's core understanding of his subject: Spies work in near darkness. They are hunters who find only fragments, or portions of fragments. It is a game with no final explanations. In *The Cardinal of the Kremlin*, the closest thing to a "proof" comes when the KGB officers do a frame-by-frame analysis of a movie taken of an event they have witnessed. Clancy cleverly underscores the point that witnessing or even participating in an event is no guarantee that the witnesses and participants will know what happened. And replaying the movie will only work if the experts are very careful.

As always, this is an author who does a superlative job of clearly rendering a nearly unfathomable subject: the high-technology of modern warfare. He lucidly explains Star Wars, its technology and the strategic rationale for such defensive weapons to counter the vast offensive nuclear arsenals of each superpower. These doses go down rather easily, and Clancy ties them nicely to the story. Experts may pick at some of his simplifications, but I think he has them about right.

CLANCY'S SOVIET SENSITIVITY

Though Clancy unfairly tilts in favor of Star Wars, there is a refreshing lack of political axe-grinding on the military. In many interviews, Clancy has wrapped himself in the flag, describing himself as an unabashed superpatriot and super-hawk. Little to none of this comes through in *The Cardinal of the Kremlin*. One might even argue that his picture of the Russians is too charitable and that Ryan has gone soft and naive when he suggests that common ground might be found between the superpowers. And Clancy's most deeply drawn and psychologically sophisticated characters are Soviets.

While Jack Ryan from *The Hunt for Red October* and *Patriot Games* is used to stitch the narrative together, *Cardinal* is by no means just his story. There are some terrific subsidiary characters. Among my favorites: the female CIA operative with the almost perfect cover, the agent aboard U.S.S. Dallas who has no past and answers no questions, and a Soviet colonel dispatched to a Soviet test site to conduct an evaluation, the ultimate recipient of which he cannot imagine.

The Cardinal of the Kremlin has a few flaws. The Washington end of the story is comparatively routine. Whenever an American journalist appears it's like a fingernail running down a blackboard; Clancy could productively spend some time with reporters learning their methods—and their ethics. In the book, the KGB does not know the identity of the CIA station chief—a near impossibility. And KGB defections can hardly be arranged as spontaneously as the one Clancy depicts.

Overall, Clancy has performed a service rare in a popular novel, one that probably will be read by millions of Americans: He has built his story around one of the chief strategic-survival questions of our time. Clancy's hero, Ryan, poses the crucial question to his fictional Soviet secretary general, Narmonov:

> You can kill most every civilian in my country, and we can murder almost every person in your country, in sixty minutes or less from the time you pick up the phone—or my President does. And what do we call that? We call it "stability."
>
> The technical name we use is MAD: Mutual Assured Destruction, which isn't even good grammar, but it's accurate enough. The situation we have now is mad, all right, and the fact that supposedly intelligent people have thought it up doesn't make it any more sensible. . . . Why do we view weapons that might protect these people to be dangerous? Isn't that backward?
>
> The damned things [nuclear weapons] are just too easy to use. You push a button, and they go, and they'll work, probably, because there's nothing to stop them. Unless something stands in their way, there's no reason to think that they won't work. And as long as somebody thinks they might work, it's too easy to use them.
>
> No, we'll never get rid of all the weapons. I know that. We'll both always have the ability to hurt each other badly, but we can make that process more complicated than it is now. We can give everybody one more reason not to push the button. That's not destabilizing, sir. That's just good sense. That's just something more to protect your conscience.

The Sum of All Fears and Clancy's Creative Accomplishment

Louis Menand

In his review of *The Sum of All Fears*, Louis Menand contends that the techno-thriller genre does not usually produce characters of a highly electric or emotional nature, but rather ones that serve a generic purpose in the overall narrative. Menand also notes that Tom Clancy's male characters tend to be much more sympathetically drawn than his female characters, who are almost always humiliated in the course of the narrative. Menand, however, points out that Clancy's incorporation of a small amount of cynicism into his characters is his one true creative accomplishment.

Louis Menand is a professor of English at the Graduate Center of the City University of New York. He has been contributing editor to the *New York Review of Books* since 1994 and is a staff writer at the *New Yorker*. With the publication of his 2002 release, *The Metaphysical Club*, he was awarded the Pulitzer Prize in history.

I counted fifty-six references to coffee in Tom Clancy's thriller, *The Sum of All Fears*. It's a long book, nearly eight hundred pages; still, that's a lot of coffee. Clancy's people need the caffeine, though, because freedom needs their vigilance. They are the intelligence analysts, fighter pilots, submariners, air-defense monitors, radar and sonar operators, secret-service agents, and other military, paramilitary, and civilian personnel on whose alertness the national security depends.

To describe Clancy's feeling for these people as respect is inadequate. He loves them; and his love includes an attentive

Louis Menand, "Very Popular Mechanics," *The New Yorker*, September 16, 1991, pp. 91–95. Copyright © 1991 by Louis Menand. Reproduced by permission.

sympathy for the special demands that a constant state of readiness, and the many cups of coffee needed to maintain it, can make. It is not unusual for one of his characters, in the midst of a sudden crisis that requires his complete concentration and on whose outcome the future of our way of life just might depend, to recall with a small but gratifying sense of relief that he has recently made a trip to the bathroom.

There is something charming about a writer who, out of sheer infatuation with his subject, is capable of this sort of unaffected tactlessness, and it will be pretty clear to most readers of *The Sum of All Fears* that whatever it is Tom Clancy has, success has done nothing to spoil it. . . .

The clearest sign of this is his abiding admiration for professionalism. His heroes are daring and manly enough, but they are not cowboys. They are organization men, highly trained, disciplined, clean-cut, and honest, men who know how to push the edge of the envelope without tearing it. They are impatient with weak authority, but disrespectful of it only when a point of personal honor is at stake—just as they are blunt and sometimes vulgar but never (by their own lights, at any rate) tasteless or cruel.

Their professionalism makes them decent. It also makes them, in spite of their wholesomeness, a little bit cynical: because they know how hard it is to live up to principles, they know how easy it is to cheat on them, and this knowledge makes them at times acutely aware that the world is probably not entirely worthy of their dedication to its survival, and that there is something faintly absurd about their insistence on maintaining such high standards of conduct.

Clancy sees—and the perception is, I think, the one genuine imaginative accomplishment of his writing—that this cynicism must be a part of the kind of characters he creates. But he cannot share it. He cannot allow virtue to be its own reward; he must allot the virtuous every earthly reward, too. And he cannot allow crimes against virtue—even the most pitiful and craven ones—to escape retribution. He wants the world to be worthy of his heroes' exertions. He knows that he is writing fairy tales, but cannot keep from begging us, like Peter Pan, to clap our hands and make it so.

PLOT SUMMARY OF *THE SUM OF ALL FEARS*

The idea in *The Sum of All Fears* is that the bad fairies have got hold of a nuclear bomb and it's up to the good fairies to keep them from starting the Third World War. The bad fairies here are a sorry group; after all, the world's supply of bad fairies has fallen off rather sharply since 1984. In *The Hunt for Red October* Clancy was able, without departing much from official attitudes, to portray the leaders of the Soviet Union as unwashed thugs, people who routinely concluded policy disputes by having the losers shot. In *The Sum of All Fears*, though, the Cold War is over, and the Soviets have become friendly and well intentioned. The Soviet military, in particular, is praised for its competence and integrity, and the Soviet President, a Gorbachev-alike called Narmonov, behaves much more nobly in the book's climactic episode than his American counterpart, a vain, ineffectual fellow (he's a liberal) called Bob Fowler.

The book begins by tidying up the one nagging trouble spot left in the new world order. It has Jack, now the deputy director of the C.I.A., whip up a peace plan for the Middle East. Jack's brainstorm is pretty simple—but then that's always the way with the really big ideas, isn't it? His plan is to evacuate the Jewish settlements on the West Bank and hand it over to the Palestinians; make Jerusalem a dominion of the Vatican governed by an interfaith troika of clerics and policed by the Swiss Guard; and guarantee Israel's security by stationing American troops there permanently. The Israelis (in an extremely feeble concession to reality) are made to have a few reservations about this plan. But the rest of the world is enthusiastic, the Israelis come to realize that it's in their interest to cooperate, and the treaty is signed by the major powers, under the vague auspices of the Pope, in a ceremony at the Vatican.

Although some people—President Fowler, for instance—
are ready to beat their swords into plowshares on the spot,
Jack knows better. As he observes during a diplomatic chat
with a Saudi prince (over coffee that is described as "thick,
bitter, and hideously strong"): "Sir, the only constant factor
in human existence is change."

Two teams of spoilers quickly (well, fairly quickly)
emerge. The first is made up of President Fowler and his
national-security adviser, a former political-science professor
from Bennington called Liz Elliot, with whom the President
happens to be sleeping. (They're both single; it's not that
kind of book.) They are weak, ambitious people who resent
Jack's brilliance and professionalism; they refuse to give him
the credit he deserves for his peace plan, and plot to drive
him out of the Administration.

The other bad fairies are a multicultural coalition of terrorists led by the notorious Qati, a fanatical anti-Zionist. His
principal cohorts are Günther, a former member of a defunct
German terrorist outfit, and Marvin, a Native American activist. Not a very impressive array of villains, you say. But
suppose these folks were to come into possession of an
atomic bomb that had been lost by the Israelis in the Golan
Heights during the 1973 war; and suppose they were to buy
the services of a former East German nuclear engineer, and
he were to use materials from that bomb to manufacture a
much more powerful hydrogen bomb; and suppose they
were to take this hydrogen bomb to Denver and try to deto-
nate it at the Super Bowl in the hope of triggering a nuclear
war between the United States and the Soviet Union—not
because that would solve the Palestinian problem or restore
the rights of Native Americans but just because they are
nasty, resentful people who, thanks in part to a series of personal disappointments, are filled with general misanthropy.
Suppose these things (and throw in a couple of submarines),
and you have supposed *The Sum of All Fears*.

For this is the most doggedly straightforward of stories.

There are no puzzles to be solved and no secrets to be uncovered. We can't completely anticipate everything that is going to happen, of course, but as soon as something does happen we are almost always told everything we need to know about it. This directness pushes events forward without distraction and serves the book well when the climactic scenes are finally reached. But it is a very long way to the climax, and for the greater part of the book the sense of slowly unravelling mystery which one associates with most spy stories and other kinds of thrillers is almost entirely absent.

This is so, I think, because Clancy appears to have, as a writer, no technical resources for producing mystery. His chief device is to report a conversation and leave out the most important part. Here, for example, is Jack Ryan coming up with his peace plan during a meeting with members of the President's staff (they're drinking Coke, by the way, which, in addition to the caffeine, provides a quick energy boost):

> "You thinking about something, Jack?" Alden asked.
> "You know, we're all 'people of the book,' aren't we?" Ryan asked, seeing the outline of a new thought in the fog.
> "So?"
> "And the Vatican is a real country, with real diplomatic status, but no armed forces . . . they're Swiss . . . and Switzerland is neutral, not even a member of the UN. The Arabs do their banking and carousing there . . . gee, I wonder if he'd go for it . . . ?" Ryan's face went blank again, and van Damm saw Jack's eyes center as the light bulb flashed on. It was always exciting to watch an idea being born, but less so when you didn't know what it was.
> "Go for what. *Who* go for *what*?" the Chief of Staff asked with some annoyance. Alden just waited.
> Ryan told them.

He doesn't tell *us*, though. It doesn't matter, since the plan is explained several chapters later and its details have no bearing on anything that happens in the interim. But it's Clancy's idea of suspense.

CHARACTER ANALYSIS

Jack himself, though he's a kind of superagent, is essentially an upright guy who's supposed to save the day without breaking the rules, and this means that he's never a particularly vivid character. One gets, for instance, almost no sense of what he looks like. It doesn't help much to learn, in one of the love scenes he's given (with his wife, and expressly for the purpose of making babies), that his hands are "strong but gentle." He is several times compared, by his nemesis Liz Elliot, to James Bond, and it's clear that we are supposed to regard the comparison as inaccurate, and an insult to Jack.

What is true of Jack is true of the rest of Clancy's people: they're cut out carefully along the dotted lines. If the story requires a professor, he will be absent-minded; if it requires a young cop, he will be gung ho and a little undisciplined. Politicians are fickle and self-serving, and reporters are jaded scandal-hounds. Asian-Americans have faith in education; Israelis are abrasive; Jesuit seminarians are more worldly-wise than they let on and don't mind sneaking a small glass of sherry before lunch.

That Clancy's world is mostly male is probably for the best, because when he creates a female character he cannot, for reasons that are not obvious to me, resist humiliating her. A female television reporter refuses to wear a bulletproof vest when she goes to interview a terrorist being staked out by the F.B.I., and when the terrorist is shot in the face and killed in front of her, his blood soaks her blouse. She is made to vomit from the shock and to rip off her shirt, "forgetting that there was nothing under it." Another woman, a convicted murderer, hangs herself in her cell after removing her dress and bra. A third, a housewife, is stripped and assassinated, and her body is sliced into pieces with a chain saw. The major female character, Liz Elliot, is grasping, contemptible, and a sexual predator. Her plots, needless to say, explode in her face, and at the end of the book her reaction to the global crisis she is supposed to help the President deal with is so hysterical that she has to be sedated.

This is all standard action-adventure stuff, no doubt, and it wouldn't be worth mentioning if it were not so unlike Clancy's treatment of his male characters. Plenty of his men die violently, and their deaths are recounted in detail that is certainly pointless enough ("The bullet entered the back of Fromm's skull, soon thereafter exiting through his forehead"), but Clancy has a kind of boyish respect for them all. Even his terrorists are accorded a certain dignity; they are, after all, by virtue of their bravery and dedication, psychotic mirror images of his heroes. But the women are punished. And not only the bad ones. Jack's wife, Cathy, though she's a crackerjack eye surgeon and supermom, is the subject of what must be one of the strangest lines ever written to conclude a love scene: "And then it was over, and he lay at her side. Cathy pulled him against her, his face to her regrettably flat chest."

USE OF TECHNOLOGY

Clancy's reputation is based not on his mastery of any of the standard storytelling techniques but on his enthusiasm for hardware: he is the inventor of the "techno-thriller." Before Clancy, technology in spy thrillers usually took the form of doomsday machines and fantastic gadgets to whose mechanics (except for guns) the hero was indifferent. ("*Try* to pay attention, 007.") What Clancy discovered when he wrote *The Hunt for Red October* was that instead of writing "The submarine started to submerge" you could write

> The reactor coolant pumps went to fast speed. An increased amount of hot, pressurized water entered the exchanger, where its heat was transferred to the steam on the outside loop. When the coolant returned to the reactor it was cooler than it had been and therefore denser.

Being denser, it trapped more neutrons in the reactor pile, increasing the ferocity of the fission reaction and giving off yet more power. Farther aft, saturated steam in the "outside" or nonradioactive loop of the heat exchange system emerged through clusters of control valves to strike the blades of the high-pressure turbine—

and people would line up to buy it.

The featured technological attraction in *The Sum of All Fears* is the nuclear bomb, of course. Many pages are devoted to its construction—there is a great deal of talk about tungstenrhenium, beryllium, gallium-stabilized plutonium, and laser interferometry—and we are treated to a slow-motion account of what happens when such a bomb goes off:

The plasma from the immolated straws pounded inward toward the second reservoir of lithium compounds. The dense uranium 238 fins just outside the Secondary pit also flashed to dense plasma, driving inward through the vacuum, then striking and compressing the tubular containment of more 238U around the central container which held the largest quantity of lithium-deuteride/tritium. The forces were immense, and the structure was pounded with a degree of pressure greater than that of a healthy stellar core.

And so on. That we are to take all this seriously is made clear by an afterword in which the author explains that "certain technical details have been altered" in order to prevent readers from trying to build nuclear bombs in their basements.

It is certainly possible that my ignorance of how submarines run and why bombs explode is even more woeful than I suspect it is; but "The plasma from the immolated straws pounded inward toward the second reservoir of lithium compounds" is actually slightly less meaningful to me than "All mimsy were the borogoves." That Clancy's sentences about nuclear technology are grammatical is one positive indication that he actually understands what he is talking about, and is not simply paraphrasing some physics text-book; but it is the only indication I feel confident about. Millions of readers obviously feel differently, and either find these descriptions illuminating or don't care that they don't.

Whether fiction helps shape the world or only reflects it is a question that is usually answered according to one's taste for the particular fiction involved. But it is interesting that among Clancy's earliest admirers in the Reagan White House were Robert McFarlane, when he was the national-security adviser, and John Poindexter, who succeeded McFarlane at the National Security Council in 1985. For *The Hunt for Red October* reads today (subject matter aside) as obviously the novel of Iran-Contra. It is fairly radiant with the conviction, so central to the belief system that made the Iran-Contra affair possible, that the national security is much too important a matter to be left to those candy-colored clowns we call the Congress; and it makes the same adolescent identification between great heroism and great secrecy which is manifest in the symbol of Iran-Contra, Oliver North.

The recent [1990–1991] war in the Persian Gulf is referred to several times in *The Sum of All Fears*, and that war, as it played on American television, was unmistakably a Tom Clancy war. The wizardly technology that turned battle into a game of reflexes, like PingPong, and the astonishingly detailed intelligence, gathered by electronic-surveillance devices that seemed able to tell us everything there was to know about the enemy until our bombs struck, but had nothing to report about the aftermath—it was all a spectacle after Clancy's own imagination. And then, interviewed as they walked to and from their amazing airplanes, there were the warriors themselves—cleancut, professional, apparently indestructible, and, ever so slightly, cynical.

Cultural Paranoia in *Debt of Honor*

Christopher Buckley

In his review of *Debt of Honor* Christopher Buckley criticizes Tom Clancy for his stereotyped and borderline racist descriptions of the Japanese. Buckley feels that Clancy is contributing to, if not creating, cultural paranoia and for a writer as popular as Tom Clancy this is nothing short of a literary crime. Buckley goes on to mock Clancy's attempt to be sensitive to feminist sensibilities, criticizing them for being unconvincing.

Buckley's main complaint, however, is that Clancy is a bad writer, and provides more than a dozen examples of what he considers weak prose.

Christopher Buckley is the author of *Thank-You for Not Smoking* and the editor of *Forbes* magazine.

Somewhere, if memory serves, Mark Twain said of one of Henry James's books, "Once you put it down, you can't pick it up." *Debt of Honor*, the eighth novel in Tom Clancy's oeuvre, is, at 766 pages, a herniating experience. Things don't really start to happen until about halfway through this book, by which time most authors, including even some turgid Russian novelists, are finished with theirs. But Tom Clancy must be understood in a broader context, not as a mere writer of gizmo-thrillers, destroyer of forests, but as an economic phenomenon. What are his editors—assuming they even exist; his books feel as if they go by modem from Mr. Clancy's computer directly to the printers—supposed to do? Tell him to cut? "You tell him it's too long." "No, you tell him."

Someone, on the other hand—friend, relative, spiritual ad-

Christopher Buckley, "Megabashing Japan," *The New York Times*, October 2, 1994, p. 28. Copyright © 1994 by *The New York Times*. Reproduced by permission.

viser, I don't know—really ought to have taken him aside and said, "Uh, Tom, isn't this book kind of racist?" I bow to no one in my disapproval of certain Japanese trade practices, and I worked for a man who once conspicuously barfed into the lap of the Japanese Prime Minister, but this book is as subtle as a World War II anti-Japanese poster showing a mustachioed Tojo bayoneting Caucasian babies. If you thought Michael Crichton was a bit paranoid, *Rising Sun*–wise, well then, to quote Mr. Clancy's favorite President and original literary booster, Ronald Reagan, "You ain't seen nothing yet." His Japanese aren't one-dimensional, they're half-dimensional. They spend most of their time grunting in bathhouses. And yet, to echo "Dr. Strangelove"'s Group Captain Lionel Mandrake, "the strange thing is, they make such bloody good cameras."

The plot: Japan craftily sabotages the United States financial markets, occupies the Mariana Islands, sinks two American submarines, killing 250 sailors, and threatens us with nuclear weapons. Why, you ask, don't we just throw up on their laps and give them a countdown to a few toasty reruns of Hiroshima and Nagasaki? Because, fools that we are, we have got rid of all our nukes in a mad disarmament pact with the Russkies. (Plausible? Never mind.)

For a while it looks like sayonara for Western civ, until Jack Ryan, now White House national security adviser, masterminds such a brilliant response to the crisis that he ends up Vice President. To make way, the current V.P. must resign because of charges of—sexual harassment. I won't be ruining it for you by saying that Ryan's ascendancy does not stop there; the President and the entire Congress must be eliminated in an inadvertently comic deus ex machina piloted by a sullen Japanese airman who miraculously does not grunt "Banzai!" as he plows his Boeing 747 into the Capitol. Former Secretary of the Navy John Lehman has recently had the arguable taste to remark, apropos this episode in *Debt of Honor*, that this particular fantasy has long been his own. I don't like Congress either, but Abraham Lincoln, Lehman's fellow Republican and mine, did go to some pains to keep the Capitol's construction going during the Civil War as a symbol of the Union's continuity. Oh, well.

CULTURAL PARANOIA

To be sure, the war enacted here is not the fruit of national Japanese will, but rather a manipulation of events by a zaibatsu businessman whose mother, father and siblings had jumped off a cliff in Saipan back in 1944 rather than be captured by evil American marines, and by a corrupt, America-hating politician. But that hardly lets Mr. Clancy off the hook, for the nasty characteristics ascribed to Yamata (the former) and Goto (the latter) are straightforwardly racial. To heat our blood further, Goto keeps a lovely American blonde as his geisha and does unspeakable naughties to her. When she threatens to become a political hot tomato, Yamata has the poor thing killed. It all plays into the crudest kind of cultural paranoia, namely, that what these beastly yellow inscrutables are really after is—our women. (A similar crime, recall, was at the heart of Mr. Crichton's novel *Rising Sun*. Well, archetypes do do the job.) Her name, for these purposes, is perfect: Kimberly Norton. "Yamata had seen breasts before, even large Caucasian breasts." To judge from the number of mentions of them, it is fair to conclude that Caucasian breasts are at the very heart of Goto-san's *Weltanschauung*. Farther down that same page, he expresses his carnal delight to Yamata "coarsely" (naturally) in—shall we say—cavorting with American girls. Jack Ryan is therefore striking a blow for more than the American way of life: he is knight-defender of nothing less than American bimbohood.

CLANCY'S FEMINISM

It must be said that the hapless Kimberly Norton is a glaring exception among Clancy women: so much so that you wonder if he's been reading Susan Faludi under the covers at night. With this book, Mr. Clancy stakes his claim to being the most politically correct popular author in America, which is somewhat remarkable in such an outspoken, if not fire-breathing, right winger as himself. Practically everyone is either black, Hispanic, a woman or, at a minimum, ethnic. The Vice President is hauled off on charges of sexual harassment; the Japanese Prime Minister is a rapist; the deputy director of operations at the C.I.A. is a woman; there is Comdr. Roberta Peach (Peach? honestly) of the Navy; Ryan's wife receives a Lasker Award for her breakthroughs in ophthalmic surgery; one of the C.I.A. assassins is informed, practically in the middle of dispatching slanty-eyed despoilers of American women, that his own daughter has made dean's list and will probably get into medical school; secretaries, we are told again and again, are the real heroes, etc., etc.

All this would be more convincing were it not for the superseding macho that permeates each page like dried sweat. Ryan's Secret Service code name is, I kid you not, "Swordsman." And there's something a bit gamey about this description of the C.I.A.'s deputy director of operations: "Mary Pat entered the room, looking about normal for an American female on a Sunday morning." His feminism, if it can be called that, is pretty smarmy, like a big guy getting a woman in a choke hold and giving her a knuckly noogie on the top of her head by way of showing her she's "O.K." (Preferable, I admit, to the entertainments offered by the officers and gentlemen of the Tailhook Association.) And there is this hilarious description of Ryan's saintly wife saving someone's sight with laser surgery: "She lined up the crosshairs as carefully as a man taking down a Rocky Mountain sheep from half a mile, and thumbed the control." You've got to admire a man who can find the sheep-hunting metaphor in retinal surgery.

CLANCY'S POOR WRITING

Tom Clancy is the James Fenimore Cooper of his day, which is to say, the most successful bad writer of his generation.

This is no mean feat, for there are many, many more rich bad writers today than there were in Cooper's time. If Twain were alive now, he would surely be writing an essay entitled, "The Literary Crimes of Clancy." He would have loved *Debt of Honor*, the culmination, thus far, of Mr. Clancy's almost endearing Hardy Boys-"Jane's Fighting Ships" prose style:

"The Indians were indeed getting frisky."

"More surprisingly, people made way for him, especially women, and children positively shrank from his presence as though Godzilla had returned to crush their city."

"'I will not become Prime Minister of my country,' Hiroshi Goto announced in a manner worthy of a stage actor, 'in order to become executor of its economic ruin.'"

"The captain, Commander Tamaki Ugaki, was known as a stickler for readiness, and though he drilled his men hard, his was a happy ship because she was always a smart ship."

"'This is better than the Concorde!' Cathy gushed at the Air Force corporal who served dinner."

"Damn, how much crazier would this world get?"

"But what kind of evil synergy was this?"

"Night at sea is supposed to be a beautiful thing, but it was not so this time."

"But I'm not a symbol, Jack wanted to tell him. I'm a man, with doubts."

"The dawn came up like thunder in this part of the world, or so the poem went."

"'I knew Goto was a fool, but I didn't think him a madman.'"

"'Gentlemen: this will work. It's just so damned outrageous, but maybe that works in our favor.'"

"'Bloody clever,' the head of the Bank of England observed to his German counterpart. 'Jawohl,' was the whispered reply."

And finally, this: "The man knew how to think on his feet, and though often a guy at the bottom of the food chain, he tended to see the big picture very clearly from down there."

Red Rabbit: An Unimaginative Novel

Edward P. Smith

In this review of *Red Rabbit*, Edward P. Smith points out the number-one problem that all techno-thriller writers have had to face, the end of the Cold War. Tom Clancy circumvents this problem by setting his 2002 novel in the early 1980s when the Berlin Wall was still in place.

Smith points out that *Red Rabbit* would have been perfectly acceptable had it been published in 1984; but that even then, Clancy's failure to include much technological gadgetry would have detracted from the book's success.

Edward P. Smith is the *Denver Post* arts and entertainment editor.

The end of the Cold War and the fall of the Soviet Union were good news for tens of millions of people. But for one very select group—the authors of spy thrillers—it definitely had its downside.

Thriller writers since have turned to terrorists, the Russian mafia and other villains in an effort to find a substitute for the Red menace. Tom Clancy, though, has come up with a different, if not particularly successful, approach. In his latest novel, *Red Rabbit*, the seminal techno-thriller author has simply turned the clock back about 20 years [to the 1980s] and pretended the Berlin Wall never fell.

GETTING PAST THE BASICS

Any critic of Clancy's books must stipulate to a few basic rules: They are a guilty pleasure best enjoyed on a beach; the

Edward P. Smith, "Spy Tale a Retreat into Past: Clancy Leaves Out What He Does Best," *The Denver Post*, August 25, 2002, p. EE-02. Copyright © 2002 by *The Denver Post*. Reproduced by permission.

writing has never been anything to, well, write home about; and the man simply refuses to leave his right-wing politics at the keyboard.

That said, Clancy's *Patriot Games*, *The Hunt for Red October* and *The Sum of All Fears* were exciting books, the gold standard for the techno-thriller genre that became so popular in the 1980s and '90s.

Some of the others were good, though maybe not quite as good as these three. His penultimate novel, *The Bear and the Dragon*, strained credulity, but it contained vivid battle scenes and, especially in the wake of the war in Afghanistan, fascinating descriptions of cutting-edge weapons and communications systems.

Red Rabbit is Clancy's effort to hold onto his franchise, but lacking any fresh ideas, he has retreated into the past. The book revisits Jack Ryan before he became director of the CIA and then president. Here he is a 32-year-old CIA analyst who has been through the terrorist attack recounted in *Patriot Games*, and has been shipped to England to spend some time honing his analytical skills with the British intelligence service.

The heart of the book is the attempted assassination of Pope John Paul II in May 1981. Clancy works off a widely held theory about the crime that suggests the KGB, through the Bulgarian intelligence service, recruited the gunman, Mehmet Ali Agca.

The motive, in Clancy's version, is that the pope has sent a secret letter to the Polish government announcing his intention to resign the papacy and return to his homeland if the authorities do not cease their efforts to suppress the Solidarity movement. Such a move would cause so much unrest throughout the Soviet Bloc, the Politburo decides, that the pope must die.

It makes for an interesting set-up, and Clancy proceeds in his usual compelling fashion to show how the KGB would go about putting such a plot together. (For a nonfiction version of this theory, see Paul Henze's *Plot to Kill the Pope* and Claire Sterling's *Time of the Assassins*.)

Complicating matters is an officer who works in the heart of the KGB's communications center. He is conscience-stricken at the thought of his government killing the pope and decides to defect with information about the plot and much more. The story revolves around efforts to remove him from Moscow and foil the attempt on the pope's life.

Ryan, of course, becomes a key player both in removing the so-called rabbit, the CIA term for a defector, from Russia and unsuccessfully trying to stop the shooter before he gets to the pope. Clancy also trots out some characters from past books, including Ed and Mary Pat Foley, the CIA uber spy couple, and James Greer, Ryan's boss at the CIA. Clancy does not try to make the pope nor the president of the day, Ronald Reagan, actual players in the drama except as offstage figures.

SOMETHING'S MISSING

This would have been a perfectly acceptable tier-two Clancy novel if it had been published in about 1984. However, in 2002 it lacks much of what makes Clancy fun. Whiz-bang technology, new weapons, futuristic eavesdropping and surveillance techniques are the things that give a good Clancy novel punch. He also can pull together a credible tale and throw in a few twists and intriguing turns.

However, in *Red Rabbit* he largely has to fall back on narrative, plot and character development. His political revelations fall into the category of telling readers what a nefarious and incompetent bunch the Politburo is. Technological innovations never get much beyond one-time cipher pads. Maybe Clancy never read any of those management books about playing to your strengths.

If you are a Tom Clancy aficionado—and you probably would not be reading this review if you were not—this probably will not make your must-read list. *Red Rabbit* is not so much an exercise in nostalgia as a lack of exercise in imagination.

Chapter 3

In His Own Words

READINGS ON
TOM CLANCY

Clancy Defends Space Exploration

Tom Clancy

Although Tom Clancy has always been a supporter of the NASA space program as a natural progression for the growth of humankind, the author also feels that the U.S. participation in space exploration was crucial in order to compete with the Soviets. At the time when this article was published, Clancy had just released *The Cardinal of the Kremlin*, a novel that depicted Soviet advances in space technology and warfare, and the implications of those advances for the United States.

Writing years before the International Space Station was operational, Tom Clancy criticized those who favored cutting NASA's funding for dooming the United States to fall behind the Soviets in a race to build a working space station. The major controversy over the idea of space exploration lies in the question, why should taxpayers' money be distributed to making advancements in a rather unknown and risky science when there are so many problems to be accounted for in this country. Tom Clancy maintains that the problems facing this country deal with social reform, and if there hasn't been any major change in twenty years, then the ability of the social reformers is in serious doubt. Clancy blames the media for playing up events like Woodstock, and other rallied efforts for social reform, while overlooking the public's interest in the space program.

Ultimately he feels space exploration is the future, and any effort to halt its progress is just a delaying of the inevitable.

On the evening of July 20 [1989], the Arts and Entertainment cable television network ran the complete coverage of the Apollo 11 moon landing and walk. It served only to refresh memories that will remain until death. Who can forget that night 20 years ago? Who can forget the pride of nationhood? Who can forget the excitement and the wonder?

MEDIA BIAS

Evidently quite a few people have chosen to do so. The media tell us that Woodstock, for example, was far more significant—despite the fact that more Americans traveled to Florida to watch Apollo 11 blast off than to have their ears blasted and their minds altered in that muddy New York pasture.

That false impression lingers to this date. It is a routine matter for hundreds of thousands of Americans to drive their cars and campers to the causeways near Cape Canaveral or the desert flatlands of California to watch the space shuttle launch and land. Yet social critics would tell us that the fact that so many American citizens make those pilgrimages is less significant than a shrill demonstration for some social issue or other—in which, of course, the media has greater interest.

Perhaps this fact demonstrates the nature of criticism, that its function is fundamentally negative, limiting—and blind. . . .

How easy it is to speak of the worthlessness of a project, how the money might be spent on some present need, how there must be better ways to do things, how we have more immediate concerns. It is the sort of vision that condemns a society to its present forever instead of leading it to the future within its grasp.

It came home to me, watching A&E that night, that the do-nothings have almost won. Watching the tapes of Neil Armstrong and Buzz Aldrin. It came home very powerfully indeed that we had wasted 20 complete years. Scarcely had the astronauts returned when NASA's funding was slashed, then slashed again. And why? To help the poor, of course. "A

nation that could go to the moon," carped those on the political left who never had any use for Apollo except as a coun-
terpoint for their own arguments, could just as easily take all
that money and solve America's crushing social problems.

FAILED SOCIAL REFORM

Well, they've had their 20 years to solve their social problems. Vast mountains of funds have been disposed of, whole
new bureaucracies created—and those who made it all happen now say that the problem is worse than ever, that we still
cannot afford a space program, that a nation that has gone to
the moon can and ought to solve its social problems first.

It was this sort of vision that made Portugal a world power.

Any decent cynic could observe that if the problems are
not solved, then the ability of the social reformers to do so is
seriously in doubt. An indecent critic might say that the War
on Poverty was fought with the same skill as that other war
[Vietnam] given us by the Johnson Administration. In either
case, deducting a few percentage points from 20 years' worth
of programs would manifestly have had no effect on the un-
solved problems at all.

But it would have given America something that the Soviet
Union has—a permanent space station where real people
could do real work. What might have come from such a facility? Who can say? You have to go there to find out.

EXPLORATION OF SPACE IS NECESSARY

Exploration is part and parcel of American history. It is said
that we ought not to go forward with a major space program
without assistance from our allies. Lewis and Clark, the first
great American explorers, traveled a land in which our European friends had little interest . . . and along the way they
discovered about a third of what we now call America. The
bread we eat comes from the region that was once called the
Great American Desert. Now we call it Kansas.

Doubtless there were pressing social problems at the time,

but it is instructive that those problems are now the subject of dry history, while the subject of the purchase and exploration are a living part of our country.

It is a fact of history that those who press outward always bring home discoveries that are useful. In simple business terms, investment in the future pays better than investment in the past. It is similarly true that you go to strange regions not for what you know is there, but for what you do not know. That's why it's called exploration. And only people can do that, because only people can look about and truly see things. Machines cannot. Exploration means people.

The one advantage in exploration that did not exist so much in earlier times is that getting there really is half the fun. The space program is the future. It really is that simple. The poor may always be with us. Certainly the naysayers will. And the future will come whether we like it or not. The question is whether or not we will be there to meet and make it. The naysayers have had their 20 years, have spent their mountains of funds and have produced slim results by their own admission. Isn't it time to give somebody else a chance?

To The Terrorists

Tom Clancy

Tom Clancy shares the patriotic values held by the heroes in his novels, and believes that most Americans hold similar values as well. Therefore, when terrorists attacked the World Trade Center and the Pentagon on September 11, 2001, Clancy felt compelled to write an open letter on behalf of all the citizens of the United States. In this letter, released just days after the attacks, Tom Clancy compares the cowardice of the terrorist group responsible (who at the time this statement was released had not been identified) to the cowardice of the Japanese who attacked Pearl Harbor on December 7, 1941. Clancy goes on to predict that those responsible for the attacks of September 11 will face a fate similar to that of the Japanese and states that it is only a matter of time before revenge will be had. Clancy invokes Japan's Admiral Isoroku Yamamoto's comparison of the United States to a sleeping dragon that was caught off guard but that it is now awake and prepared to unleash a hellish fury. Above all, Clancy expresses his confidence in America's military forces and their ability to defend their country.

It was a friend of mine formerly of the Royal Navy who first pointed out that the casualty count on this incident exceeds that of Pearl Harbour.

Yes, my country has taken a big and costly hit, and somewhere, perhaps in South Asia, some people are exchanging high-fives and having themselves a good laugh. And maybe they're entitled to it. Like Pearl Harbour, it was a well planned and well executed black operation. But, you know, they've made the same mistake that Japan made back in 1941.

Tom Clancy, "We're Going to Get You," *Associated Newspapers*, September 16, 2001. Copyright © 2001 by Tom Clancy. Reproduced by permission.

It's remarkable to me that America is so hard for some people to understand. We are the most open of books, after all. Our values and customs are portrayed on TV and movie screens all over the world. Is the character of my country so hard to grasp?

Japan figured that they could defeat us not physically, but morally, that America was not tough enough to defeat their death-seeking warriors, that we would be unwilling to absorb the casualties. (In this they were right: we didn't absorb all the casualties they tried to inflict but that was because we killed their samurai much more efficiently than they were able to kill our men.) An enemy willing to die in the performance of his duty can indeed be a formidable adversary, but, you see, we've dealt with such people before. They die just like everyone else.

A SOLDIER'S PROFESSIONALISM

Perhaps the American sort of patriotism, like the British sort, just isn't bombastic enough for our enemies to notice.

We don't parade about thumping our chests and proclaiming how tough we are, whereas other people like that sort of display.

But they don't seem to grasp the fact that they do it because they have to; they evidently need to prove to themselves how formidable they are.

Instead, our people, like yours, train and practise their craft every day, out in the field at places like Fort Bragg, North Carolina, and Fort Irwin, California.

I've been to both places and seen our people and how they train. The difference between a civilian or a common ruffian and a soldier, you see, is training.

A professional soldier is as serious about his work as a surgeon is about his. Such people are not, in my experience, boastful. If you ask what they can do, they will explain it to you, usually in quiet tones, because they do not feel the need to prove anything. Off duty they are like everyone else, watching football on TV and enjoying a quiet beer with their pals. They read books, shop at the local supermarkets, and mow the grass at home. They all enjoy a good laugh. They make the best of friends.

They look physically fit and indeed they are physically fit because their job requires it, and every day they do something tiresome in the field, working at some more or less demanding field exercise, again and again and again until every aspect of their job is as automatic as zipping one's zipper is for us people in civilian life.

But, you know, inside all of these people, such as the 82nd Airborne at Fort Bragg, or the 75th Ranger Regiment at Fort Steward, Georgia, there burns a little flame.

Not a big one; instead like the pilot light in a gas stove. And when you put more gas there, the flame gets bigger, enough to cook with.

Inside every one of these people is something else, something you have to look for: pride. They know that they are good at their work, in the event they ever have to do it for real. This doesn't happen very often, and indeed they do not ordinarily lust to do it because it's a serious, nasty job. The job is the taking of life.

Military organisations exist for only one mission: killing people and breaking things. This is not something to be undertaken lightly, because life is a gift from God, and a lot of these people, kids, really, can be found in church on Sunday mornings. But their larger purpose, the reason these kids enlist, both in my country and in yours, is to preserve, protect, and defend their nations and the citizens who live there.

It's not an easy job, but someone has to do it, and typically the hardest jobs attract the best of us.

Mostly they never have to kill anybody, and that's okay with them. It's knowing that they are able to do something difficult and dangerous that gives them their pride.

This purpose, defending their country, is something they don't talk much about, but it's always there, and with it comes a quiet, steely look in the eyes. Especially when something like this happens.

That's when their sense of self is insulted, and these are people who do not bear insults well.

They are protectors, and when those whom they are sworn to protect are hurt, then comes the desire and the lust to perform their mission. Even then it's quiet.

They will not riot or pose before TV cameras or cry aloud for action, because that's not their way. They are the point of the lance, the very breath of the dragon, and at times like this they want to know the taste of blood.

Their adversaries just don't appreciate what they are capable of. It's something too divorced from their experience. This isn't like hosing civilians with your machine gun or setting off a bomb somewhere, or killing unarmed people strapped and helpless inside a commercial aircraft.

This means facing professional warriors at a time and place of their choosing, and that is something terrorists don't really prepare for.

The day of Pearl Harbour, the commander of the Japanese navy told his staff not to exult too much, that all their beautifully executed operation had accomplished was to awaken a sleeping dragon and give it a dreadful purpose.

Perhaps alone in his country, Isoroku Yamamoto, who had lived briefly in America, knew what his enemy was capable of, and for that reason, perhaps he was not surprised when the .50-calibre bullet from a P-38 fighter entered his head and ended his life.

Whoever initiated last week's operation is probably not quite as appreciative of what he has begun as Yamamoto was. Because the dragon is now fully awake, and its breath is too hot for men to bear.

America is now fully awake. Our quiet patriotism is a little louder now, but it will not get too loud.

Why spoil the surprise?

Is the CIA to Blame for the September 11, 2001, Attacks?

Tom Clancy

In this editorial published a week after the terrorist attacks of September 11, 2001, Tom Clancy decries the public and media criticism of the government's intelligence agencies for their purported failure to prevent the attacks. Clancy criticizes the American media for feeding public sentiment against the CIA prior to September 11, 2001, and then blaming the agency for failing to prevent the attacks. The CIA, Clancy points out, was created to gather information. It is up to whoever is sitting in the White House and Congress to interpret and utilize that information for the nation's defense.

Clancy also classifies an act of terrorism as a political act, the objective of which is to force change in the targeted society through shock. Clancy goes on to suggest that America should take the supposed intelligence failure as a lesson and not cripple the nation's intelligence capability in the future.

We know now that America has been the victim of a large, well-planned, and well-executed terrorist act. The parameters are yet to be fully explored, but that won't stop the usual suspects from pontificating (and, yes, that includes me) on what happened and what needs to be done as a result. A few modest observations:

• As I write this we only know the rough outlines of what has taken place. We do not know exactly who the perpetra-

Tom Clancy, "First We Cripple the CIA, Then We Blame It," *The Wall Street Journal*, September 18, 2001. Copyright © 2001 by Tom Clancy. Reproduced by permission.

tors were, though we have heard from Vice President Dick Cheney that there is "no question" that Osama bin Laden had a role. But many groups may have been involved, and we do not know their motivation, or for whom or for what particular objective they worked.

• "Don't know" means "don't know" and nothing more. Absent hard information, talking about who it must have been and what we need to do about it is a waste of air and energy. To discern the important facts, we have the Federal Bureau of Investigation as our principal investigative agency, and the Central Intelligence Agency (along with National Security Agency and the Defense Intelligence Agency) as our principal foreign-intelligence services. Getting the most important information is their job, not the job of the news media, which will only repeat what they are told. Gathering this information will take time, because we need to get it right.

• Terrorism is a political act, performed for political objectives. The general aim of terrorism is to force changes in the targeted society through the shock value of the crime committed. Therefore, if we make radical changes in how our country operates, the bad guys win. We do not want that to happen. Whoever planned this operation is watching us right now, and they are probably having a pretty good laugh. We can't stop that. What we can do is to maintain that which they most hate, which is a free society. We've worked too hard to become what we are; and we can't allow a few savages to change it for us.

Next, our job is to take a step back, take a deep breath and get to work finding out who it was, where they are, and what to do about it.

IMPORTANCE OF THE CIA

Terrorism is a crime under the civil law when committed by domestic terrorists; it can be an act of war when committed by foreigners. For domestic criminals we have the FBI and police. For acts of war we have our intelligence community and the military. In either case we have well-trained people to do the work. If we let them do their job, and give them the support they need, the job will get done as reliably as gravity. The foreign-source option seems the most likely at this time. The first line of defense in such a case is the intelligence community. The CIA is an agency of about 18,000 employees, of whom perhaps 800 are field-intelligence officers—that is, the people who go out on the street and learn what people are thinking, not how many tanks they have parked outside (we have satellites to photograph those).

I've been saying for a lot of years that this number is too small. American society doesn't love its CIA, for the same reason that it doesn't always love its cops. We too often regard them as a threat to ourselves rather than our enemies. Perhaps these incidents will make us rethink that.

The best defense against terrorist incidents is to prevent them from happening. You do that by finding out what a potential enemy is thinking before he is able to act. What the field intelligence officers do is no different from what Special Agent Joe Pistone of the FBI did when he infiltrated the mafia under the cover name of Donnie Brasco. The purpose of these operations is to find out what people are thinking and talking about. However good your satellites are, they cannot see inside a human head. Only people can go and do that.

AMERICAN MEDIA CRIPPLES THE CIA

But America, and especially the American news media, does not love the CIA in general and the field spooks in particular. As recently as two weeks ago, CBS's "60 Minutes" regaled us with the hoary old chestnut about how the CIA undermined the leftist government of Chile three decades ago [early 1970s]. The effect of this media coverage, always solicitous to leftist governments, is to brand the CIA an antiprogressive agency that does Bad Things.

In fact, the CIA is a government agency, subject to the political whims of whoever sits in the White House and Congress. The CIA does what the government of which it is a part tells it to do. Whatever evil the CIA may have done was the result of orders from above. . . .

It is a lamentably common practice in Washington and elsewhere to shoot people in the back and then complain when they fail to win the race. The loss of so many lives in New York and Washington is now called an "intelligence failure," mostly by those who crippled the CIA in the first place, and by those who celebrated the loss of its invaluable capabilities.

What a pity that they cannot stand up like adults now and say: "See, we gutted our intelligence agencies because we don't much like them, and now we can bury thousands of American citizens as an indirect result." This, of course, will not happen, because those who inflict their aesthetic on the rest of us are never around to clean up the resulting mess, though they seem to enjoy further assaulting those whom they crippled to begin with.

Call it the law of unintended consequences. The intelligence community was successfully assaulted for actions taken under constitutionally mandated orders, and with nothing left to replace what was smashed, warnings we might have had to prevent this horrid event never came. Of course, neither I nor anyone else can prove that the warnings would have come, and I will not invoke the rhetoric of the political left on so sad an occasion as this.

But the next time America is in a fight, it is well to remember that tying one's own arm is unlikely to assist in preserving, protecting and defending what is ours.

CHAPTER 4

Rebuilding an American Hero: The Appeal of Tom Clancy

READINGS ON
TOM CLANCY

Tom Clancy and the Cult of National Security

Walter L. Hixson

Historian Walter L. Hixson writes that Tom Clancy's novels depend on assumptions typical of the Reagan-era White House, what Hixson calls the cult of national security. Hixson goes on to note that like Reagan and those who surrounded him, Clancy's novels promote the myth of Americans as being morally, politically, and technologically superior. Just as important as America's triumph over its enemies is the means by which it triumphs. Hixson concludes that Clancy's first three novels not only hinge on the cult of national security, but help to promote that mentality, especially since President Reagan himself publicly praised *The Hunt for Red October*.

Walter L. Hixson is an associate professor of history at the University of Akron. He is the author of *Witness to Disintegration: Provincial Life in the Last Year of the USSR* (1993) and is working on a study of U.S.-Soviet cultural relations in the late 1950s.

The best-selling novels of Tom Clancy, the most popular writer of *any* type of fiction in the 1980s, with sales of more than thirty million books in the United States alone, show how fruitful research into [the techno-thriller] genre can be. Three of Clancy's novels—*The Hunt for Red October, Red Storm Rising*, and *The Cardinal of the Kremlin*—can be interpreted as popular representations of Reagan-era Cold War values. They reflect both popular perceptions of Soviet behavior and the predominant national security values of the

Walter L. Hixson, "Red Storm Rising: Tom Clancy Novels and the Cult of National Security," *Diplomatic History*, vol. 17, Fall 1993, pp. 599–613. Copyright © 1993 by Blackwell Publisher Ltd. Reproduced by permission.

Reagan era. They also perpetuate myths about the American past and reinforce the symbols, images, and historical lessons that have dominated Cold War discourse. . . .

THE CULT OF NATIONAL SECURITY

Clancy's novels hinge on what might be called the cult of national security, a set of assumptions and policy formulations to which the Reagan administration adhered. Reviving orthodox perceptions of the early Cold War, Reagan administration national security planners embraced worst-case scenarios of Soviet behavior based on the assumption of the existence of a totalitarian regime bent on global expansion and, ultimately, "world domination." They perceived the USSR as beyond reform and utterly cynical with respect to the means it might employ to achieve its aggressive design. The cult of national security arrogated to Washington the primary responsibility to contain and deter the Soviet Union, thus invoking a language that reinforced the Cold War preoccupation with the adversary's capabilities rather than its intentions. National security policy also sanctioned intervention on behalf of authoritarian regimes, using, once again, the words containment and deterrence—defensive terms that implied that Washington actually sought to promote self-determination. The cult of national security mandated strict control over foreign policy by the executive branch of government and sought to manage or subvert, sometimes through covert, illegal, or constitutionally questionable means, congressional and public opposition. Adherents of the cult of national security equated negotiation with Communist adversaries with Munich-style appeasement and sought to discredit domestic proponents of détente.

Clancy's texts, like the Reagan administration itself, not only reflected the cult of national security but apotheosized the American dream as well. Indeed, Clancy's own rise from Maryland insurance salesman to best-selling author and newsweekly cover star rivals any Horatio Alger tale. His six (through 1992) espionage and national security novels all topped the best-seller list for months and were translated into several languages, making him arguably the most widely read author in the Western world. Hollywood converted both *The Hunt for Red October* and *Patriot Games* into commercially successful films.

INVOCATION OF AMERICAN MYTHOLOGY

What accounts for the mass appeal of Clancy's novels? Even some of his most avid readers admit that the books do not thrive on literary merit. Clancy may be a more accomplished stylist than [mystery writer Mickey] Spillane, but just barely. Critics have called attention to his "undistinguished prose"; "wooden dialogue"; "plastic characters . . . on a Victorian boy's book level"; and "rubber-band plot[s] that stretch credibility to the breaking point." Although Clancy sometimes succeeds in building suspense toward a page-turning climax—the elementary requirement of the genre—even in this respect he is no Frederick Forsyth. "If you don't share Clancy's reverence for the spectacle of a gigantic national-security apparatus mobilizing to repel foreign evildoers," noted critic Terrence Rafferty, "[Clancy's] stories are just a bore—you settle back in the bulletproof limo, close your eyes, and try to shut out the driver's jabbering."

Rather than thriving on their literary merit, it seems likely that Clancy's novels sell at least in part for the same reasons that Ronald Reagan was an immensely popular president. Much as Reagan did, Clancy rewards the public by invoking powerful themes that are embedded in the American cultural tradition. Perhaps the most potent theme invoked by both Reagan and Clancy is the enduring mythology of American exceptionalism—moral, political, and technological. In all three novels analyzed below, the American heroes—invariably patriotic white males employed by the nation's military or intelligence services—are virtuous products of a materially successful pluralist democracy. As yet another critic has noted, "What Clancy has to offer—and it makes his books emblematic of the Reagan administration's self-image—is an old-fashioned sense of certitude, righteousness and derring-do." Clancy's patriotic heroes are highly skilled, disciplined, honest, thoroughly professional, and only lose their cool when incompetent politicians or bureaucrats get in their way. Their unambiguous triumphs over evil provide symbolic relief from the legacy of the Vietnam War, the country's most recent actual conflict, in which military victory proved illusive and distinctions between good and evil proved illusory. There are numerous parallels between Reagan and Clancy. Clancy buries the legacy of Vietnam, just as Reagan attempted to do. Like Reagan, Clancy evokes nostalgic memories of American innocence and military victory in World War II, the "good war" in which the United States (the critical role played by its allies, especially the Soviet Union, having been minimized in U.S. cultural discourse) defeated Hitler as well as the "Japs" and enjoyed unparalleled security through its monopoly on atomic weapons. Clancy's texts thus complement the "Dr. Feel-good" Reagan era in that they succeed in reinvesting American culture with nostalgic images of military victory over external demons, and they resist accommodation to a new status of "relative decline" in world affairs.

Clancy's novels reinforce American exceptionalism by demonizing both foreign enemies and domestic political foes, much as the Reagan administration did also. . . .

The Clancy novels employ Stalinist imagery, for the same reason Reagan did, to demonize the Soviet "evil empire" while promoting the mythology of American exceptionalism and the cult of national security. Clancy's demonization of the USSR and manichean imagery reflect a pattern of countersubversive behavior that has been embedded in American culture since colonial literature reduced the frontier to a struggle between the Indian savage and the hunter hero. The Clancy novels demonize not only the external enemy but the internal one as well. Because the stories reflect and promote one conception of national security, they vilify American liberals, academics, homosexuals, the news media, and other putative challengers of the Cold War ethos. Like past proponents of red scare hysteria over internal security, Clancy's novels suggest that the United States could be undermined from within by spies and dupes of the international Communist conspiracy.

ROLE OF TECHNOLOGY

The triumph of American virtue only partially accounts for the appeal of Clancy's novels; equally important is *how* the heroes of his fiction triumph. Clancy's novels attach great importance to salvation through technology. John Buchan's hero used only his own ingenuity to overcome evil doers. Although James Bond did employ deadly gadgets to get himself out of tight spots, he disdained being briefed about them (*"Try* to pay attention, 007!"*) and never used them to achieve the ultimate conquest of his adversary. Clancy, on the other hand, a self-confessed "technology freak" with a sure grasp of military hardware, has made his mark as "king of the technothriller." Virtually without exception American weapons—from nuclear submarines to the Stealth fighter to SDI [Strategic Defense Initiative]—work unerringly and are decisive in the final resolution of his plots. Consistent with Reagan's promotion of such programs as the MX "Peacekeeper" missile and SDI, Clancy's texts encourage the view that bolstering strategic arsenals, far from posing a threat to human existence, will enable the nation to deter and if necessary defeat aggressors as it fulfills its role as the exceptional guarantor of world order.

THE HUNT FOR RED OCTOBER

Clancy's first and perhaps best-crafted novel, *The Hunt for Red October* (1984), contains all these elements—an emphasis on American exceptionalism, demonized enemies, and an array of high-tech weaponry. The enduring appeal of the book stems in part from its success as a classic thriller. It is, one reviewer noted, "the most satisfactory novel of a sea chase since C.S. Forester perfected the form." The plot centers on the defection of a Soviet captain (Marko Ramius) to the United States in his nation's most advanced nuclear submarine while the Soviet navy gives chase and American officials try to clear his path. Despite the privileges that accrue to the Soviet navy's top submarine pilot, Ramius chooses to defect because he had begun to question Communist orthodoxies, and indeed had become "an individual in his thinking, and so unknowingly committed the gravest sin in the Communist pantheon [*sic*]."

Thus, the first forty pages of the novel establish the demonic nature of the USSR as the reader begins to identify with a Soviet protagonist who is exceptional because he acts as an individual in a regimented society founded on terror. (According to Clancy, the Soviet Union of the mid-1980s was still a state in which the KGB could "order the execution or imprisonment of a hundred men without blinking.") In contrast to the redoubtable Ramius, most Soviet characters in *Red October* are dull-witted true believers in Marxism-Leninism. Clancy's American characters refer to the average Russian as "Ivan," evoking a more "terrible" image than does the noble-sounding Ramius, who is a Baltic European.

While the Soviet characters bumble their way toward strategic defeat, Jack Ryan and his colleagues skillfully guide *Red October* to U.S. shores, pulling off the whole enterprise so that neither the Soviets nor the American public are even aware of it. The novel highlights a U.S. intelligence operation that is both covert and successful, thus reassuring readers that their intelligence services may be accomplishing great things without their knowledge. U.S. intelligence services, the story suggests, should be amply funded and given license to conduct their business without the burden of external oversight. During the Iran-contra imbroglio, the Reagan administration showed that it shared the same view.

Through the character of Peter Henderson, Clancy underscores the dangers of democratic oversight while demonizing opponents of the national security cult. After progressing from Harvard, where he was an editor on the *Crimson* as well as an activist against the Vietnam War, Henderson became an aide to a U.S. senator and a KGB spy. The Henderson character alerts the reader to the dangers of congressional oversight by suggesting that congressmen may unwittingly pass information through disloyal aides into the hands of the tireless agents of international communism. Moreover, Henderson's character suggests that those who were involved in the antiwar movement and those with "liberal East Coast" and "liberal media" connections are potential traitors.

Despite the Henderson-Hiss-Lattimore attempts to stab America in the back, the mission succeeds, Ramius gains freedom, and Jack Ryan trumpets U.S. exceptionalism and material abundance. He informs a group of incredulous Russians that the United States is a land of unparalleled material wealth and equal opportunity. "Anything you want. . . . Beef, pork, lamb, turkey, chicken. . . . The United States feeds itself and has plenty left over. . . . Everyone has a car. Most people own their own homes. . . . The fact of the matter is that in our country if you have some brains . . . and you are willing to work . . . you will live a comfortable life even without any help." Moments later, Mannion, a black U.S. sailor, informs Ramius that all the Soviet propaganda he has heard about racism and the white bourgeois ruling class in America is just that—propaganda. Much like the Reagan administration itself, Clancy's characters dealt with poverty and racial inequality by acting as if they did not exist.

RED STORM RISING

While demonization of the Soviet Union is an important element of *The Hunt for Red October*, it plays an even greater role in Clancy's second work, *Red Storm Rising* (1986). As the title image suggests, the novel emphasizes naked Soviet military aggression against the West. More than any other Clancy novel, *Red Storm Rising* promotes the worst-case scenarios of Soviet military behavior upon which the cult of national security depended. The book begins with dark-skinned, Koran-toting, Allah-quoting Soviet Muslim fanatics sabotaging a huge Siberian oil refining complex, thus depriving the USSR of 34 percent of its crude oil production and risking an internal rebellion on the part of "the faceless collection of men and women who toiled every day . . . in factories and on collective farms, their thoughts hidden behind unsmiling masks." The Soviet defense minister declares at an emergency Politburo meeting that "we must obtain more oil. It is as simple as that." Because not enough can be purchased, he concludes that "we must take it." The plot of *Red Storm Rising* thus reinforces the nightmarish image of an unstable totalitarian state that might at any moment resort to foreign "adventurism" to solve problems that flow from domestic instability. Like the Soviet bear, a large and powerful beast with a primitive mentality, Soviet leaders are violent and unpredictable. "In the Politburo, as in the jungle," the narrator avers, "the only rule was survival."

While the West is lulled to sleep by the détente line promoted by the new Communist party general secretary, the real decisions are being made in the Defense Ministry, which opts for total war to secure Soviet dominance of Europe and the Persian Gulf. Thus, the Politburo votes overwhelmingly (in the midst of a failed campaign in neighboring Afghanistan) to risk nuclear war by seizing the Persian Gulf after first launching an all-out invasion of NATO-occupied Western Europe. The Hitlerian nightmare unfolds with a reprise of Munich, as the Kremlin leadership trumpets détente before the world community and even proposes a 50 percent reduction, with verification, of superpower nuclear arsenals.

After encouraging appeasement in the West, the Soviets initiate hostilities in the most cynical fashion—by killing innocent *Soviet* children in a Kremlin explosion and blaming it on West Germany, which they then invade. After neutralizing Europe, the Red Army extends its *blitzkrieg* by invading Iceland in order to seize control of the Atlantic. Soviet storm troopers smash the tiny, nonviolent country, which is defended only by a national police force.

During the Icelandic invasion, Soviet soldiers kill the mother, father, and dog of a young—and of course pregnant—Icelandic woman, who is herself subjected to a gang rape. The rape and the subsequent rescue scene revive a narrative formula first popularized by James Fenimore Cooper's Leatherstocking tales and cemented in American cultural discourse ever since. The Cooperian mythology revolves around scenes of captivity, savagery, and violent regeneration through the heroism of the solitary hunter. In this case the solitary hunter is Mike Edwards, an air force lieutenant stationed at a NATO outpost on the western coast of Iceland. Like the self-made men who "tamed the frontier" before him, Edwards is not by nature a violent man, but even the mild-mannered air force meteorologist is compelled to adopt the savage frontier ethos. Sickened by the brutal rape and murders, Edwards and his fellow GIs cannot restrain themselves from summarily executing the Soviet prisoners who committed the atrocities. (The Icelandic woman falls in love with Edwards two days after being gang-raped.) The Russian soldiers thus merge with Spillane's "red sons of bitches" and with the savage Indians, Filipino "goo-goos," "Huns," "Japs," Nazis, and Vietnamese "gooks" as barbaric enemies who must be exterminated.

The Stealth fighter and bomber aircraft represent the theme of salvation through strategic technology in *Red Storm Rising*. "We nearly defeated you," the defeated Soviet General Alekseyev explains. "If those damned invisible bombers of yours hadn't hit our bridges on the first day, or if we had managed to smash three or four of your convoys, you would be offering me terms."

THE CARDINAL OF THE KREMLIN

After drawing sharper criticism from reviewers of his third novel, *Patriot Games*, a tale about IRA terrorist attempts to seize the British royal family, Clancy returned to the Soviet enemy in *The Cardinal of the Kremlin* (1988). Like *Red Storm Rising*, *Cardinal* opens with a reprise of an Allah-quoting, Koran-toting Afghani Muslim fanatic (with "dark pitiless eyes") gunning down Soviet soldiers in the mountains of Azerbaijan, where the Kremlin's operation Bright Star, an SDI-type system, is under construction. As Americans and Soviets seek to learn about and sabotage each other's SDI programs, a top CIA asset high in the Soviet defense ministry, Mikhail S. Filitov—the Cardinal of the Kremlin—is exposed and jailed and the top U.S. SDI scientist is kidnapped. The heroic Jack Ryan, aided by the *mujahideen* in Afghanistan (depicted as "freedom fighters" rather than Koran-toting fanatics), allows the United States to rescue its kidnapped scientist and free the Cardinal himself.

The Cardinal of the Kremlin promotes SDI as the means to salvation through technological advance. "Defense systems could not be stopped now," Filitov observes. "One might as easily try to stop the tide." The Soviet character Yazov obligingly confirms the Reagan administration line when he acknowledges that his country is not only deeply involved in research on strategic defensive systems but is also "further along in testing." Soviet negotiating offers, especially with respect to arms control, are dismissed as disingenuous ploys that mask malevolent intent. Only dupes in Congress and liberal peaceniks could think otherwise.

Like the rape and rescue scenes in *Red Storm Rising*, a demonization scene in *Cardinal* features Soviet savagery, this time directed at a beautiful Soviet woman who is an American spy. (Beautiful Soviet women are American spies; most Soviet women are depicted in Cold War popular culture as overweight matrons, like the uniformed comrade in the popular Wendy's television commercial that appeared in the late

1980s.) Following her capture, the blonde woman makes a drug-induced confession as the Nazi-like doctor caresses her naked body. Mind-altering drugs make her forget everything. The Nazi-Soviet doctor later explains: "Surely you have read *1984.* It might have been a dream when Orwell wrote it, but with modern technology we can do it." Invoking the most clichéd totalitarian imagery, the narrator describes the brainwashed woman's once animated face as "blank. What had been lively was now as emotionless as any face on a Moscow street." Big Brother no longer even needed to watch her. The imagery of totalitarian robotization is reinforced in other passages, where readers learn that Russians are "so grim all the time" (in part because their smiles "stop at their lips"); they don't "know how to have a good time"; and they themselves even admit that they "should have more Americans around."

EFFECT OF CLANCY'S NOVELS ON THE AMERICAN PERSONA

This brief summary of the three Clancy novels shows the extent to which his popular fiction embodies the predominant national security values of the Reagan administration. Clancy's evocation of American exceptionalism, demonization of the Soviet Union, and his promotion of the national security *mentalité* indicate how deeply the United States invested in the language and symbols of the Cold War during the Reagan years. In the wake of defeat in Vietnam, the Watergate scandal, revelations of CIA misconduct, and the crises of the Carter years, Americans yearned to replace the morally ambiguous legacies of the Cold War with the unambiguous triumph of good over evil. Both Reagan's presidency and Clancy's novels were means to that end.

While the symbiosis between Clancy's texts and Reagan-era Cold War values seems clear, it is more difficult to assess the extent to which the books actually reinforced and promoted those values. It is not unreasonable to assume that the stress upon American exceptionalism, the demonization of the USSR, and the depiction of salvation through military technology reinforced the cult of national security in the minds of millions of Clancy readers. Clancy's novels, like those of Mickey Spillane, became best sellers in the same period that East-West tensions reached a new peak. It seems likely, therefore, that Clancy's fiction, like the Spillane novels of the early 1950s, helped bolster the Cold War ethos through the medium of popular culture.

The efforts of national security elites to promote Clancy's books, movies, and the author himself offer the best evidence that his popular fiction played a meaningful role in shaping opinion in the real world. The military establishment at first expressed some concern over Clancy's sure grasp of "secret" military technology, but it quickly concluded that such concerns were trivial when measured against the "great service" that Clancy's books performed by promoting the interests of the armed services and the military-industrial complex. Accordingly, the military establishment "adopted me," as Clancy himself once put it, by providing the popular author with privileged access to restricted facilities, job offers, and promotion of his books and films. "Everybody's willing to talk to Clancy," observed a Pentagon spokesman. "He's neat. He's one of the good guys." A Ford Foundation critic complained that leaks to Clancy were "the authorized winked-at way to leak information that will help the military procurement budget." Republican national strategist Edward Rollins and representative Newt Gingrich of Georgia found Clancy such an effective spokesman for the cult of national security that they urged him to challenge Maryland representative Roy Dyson, a prominent Democrat on the House Armed Services Committee, in 1992. Clancy declined. . . .

The official embrace of *The Hunt for Red October* extended to the White House, where Clancy dined with the Reagans. Indeed, *The Hunt for Red October* became a publishing phenomenon only after Reagan called it "the perfect yarn" and recommended it to the nation. Senators, including

Dan Quayle, who was then a senator from Indiana, praised Clancy, not as a novelist but as an authority on national security. During a debate on funding of anti-satellite weapons (ASAT) technology, Quayle held Clancy's *Red Storm Rising* aloft on the Senate floor and asked, "Have you read this book? ASAT technology is what wins the war!"

The reception accorded Clancy's novels in these circles makes it clear that national security elites exploited his popular fiction to promote the cult of national security. Millions of readers have absorbed Clancy's exaltation of American exceptionalism, demonization of foreign and domestic political enemies, and promotion of military technology and new weapons systems. One cannot conclusively prove that Clancy's novels reinforced or changed the way those readers thought about the Cold War or U.S. foreign policy any more than one can "prove" that the Truman Doctrine or John F. Kennedy's inaugural address shaped public perceptions about the Cold War. What can be demonstrated, in this case, is that Clancy's novels promoted ideologically constructed perceptions of foreign policy discourse—perceptions that were absorbed by millions of Americans and were actively promoted by a national security establishment whose interests they served.

Tom Clancy's Moral Seriousness

Walter Shapiro

In this review of *Clear and Present Danger*, Walter Shapiro defends Tom Clancy from critics who dismiss him as a writer of potboilers. Shapiro commends the patriotism and passion underlying Clancy's writing; he calls *Clear and Present Danger* Clancy's most philosophically complex novel. Shapiro also notes that in the characterization of Jack Ryan, a possible alter ego who shares Clancy's morality, civic-mindedness, and affluence, the author has created a self-confident persona that only helps to establish his legacy as one of the most valuable entertainers in mass-market fiction.

At the time he wrote this viewpoint, Walter Shapiro was a senior writer for *Time* magazine.

What an exhausting five-year run [1984–1989] it has been for backwater insurance agent turned blockbuster novelist Tom Clancy. Forget the four straight best sellers published since 1984 and the 20 million copies sold. Forget the movie version of his first novel [*The Hunt for Red October*] now in production. Forget the $4 million advance for his thriller *Clear and Present Danger.* Forget such crass calculus of cash-register commerce.

Dwell instead on what this chain-smoking, nearsighted, 42-year-old family man with a hyperactive imagination has boldly orchestrated on the global stage. It would have been enough that he engineered the defection of a Soviet nuclear submarine in *The Hunt for Red October.* But no, Clancy had

Walter Shapiro, "Of Arms and the Man," *Time*, August 21, 1989, pp. 66–68.

to go fight World War III without firing a single nuclear weapon in *Red Storm Rising*—and make sure that the good guys narrowly won.

Then there was *Patriot Games*, where Clancy's plucky hero Jack Ryan just happened to be in London in time to rescue two royals, seemingly Prince Charles and Lady Di, from a terrorist attack, and, of course, was rewarded with a knighthood from a grateful Queen. Call that just vacation fun compared with what Clancy pulled off in *The Cardinal of the Kremlin*. Not only did he virtually save the job of a reform-minded Soviet leader but he also spirited a defecting KGB chief onto Air Force One to fly to the land of freedom, opportunity and new Tom Clancy novels.

This time around, in writing *Clear and Present Danger*, Clancy got mad. Not at his usual villains, like the Soviets or international terrorists. Instead, what aroused his ire was what the Iran-*contra* affair revealed about "how the Government makes decisions, what kind of people make those decisions, and what happens when things go wrong." That is what settling insurance claims teaches: how often in real life things go wrong. And when that happens to soldiers and spooks, Clancy says, "very often you get hung out to dry. All those Marines who got blown up in Lebanon got hung out to dry. William Buckley, the CIA officer who got captured by the bad guys in Beirut, was hung out to dry. We do that a lot; it's probably the most despicable thing our Government can do. But it happens, and that's what I decided to write about."

The book that arose out of these emotions is Clancy's most politically sophisticated and philosophically complex. (Beach readers, have no fear; this is not Sartre.) There are no direct references to Iran-*contra*, no arms-for-hostages deals and no Ollie Norths; Clancy is too accomplished a craftsman for such overt gambits. The closest parallel comes in the fictional National Security Adviser, Vice Admiral James Cutter, who is reminiscent of John Poindexter. Almost from the moment the admiral is introduced, readers can sense Clancy's scorn: "Cutter was the sort of sailor for whom the sea was a means to an end. More than half of his career had been spent in the Pentagon, and that . . . was no place for a proper sailor."

THE PLOT OF *A CLEAR AND PRESENT DANGER*

Clancy's intricate plot begins with Cutter's winning presidential approval for a covert operation against the Colombian drug cartel. The ill-conceived plan: insert four platoons of élite U.S. Army light infantrymen into the Colombian jungle to identify drug-running planes and disrupt cocaine production. With his trademarked obsession for military detail and shrewd insights into the psyches of fighting men, Clancy recounts the training of Sergeant "Ding" Chavez and the other "light-fighters" (fast-moving small units unencumbered by heavy equipment) for their quasi-legal mission.

Almost as soon as Chavez and his fellow grunts hit the ground, things begin to go awry. Big things, like the assassination of the FBI director on a secret visit to Bogotá. Before long, U.S. pilots are dropping untraceable bombs (dubbed "Hush-A-Bombs") on the fortified castles of the Colombian drug lords, while Chavez and his compatriots are hung out to dry—abandoned in the jungle on Cutter's orders.

It should come as scant surprise to connoisseurs of Clancy's earlier novels that along about now the sometimes cloyingly straight-arrow CIA man Jack Ryan mounts a daring maneuver to rescue the light-fighters. There are other familiar Clancy touches. While the author has moved beyond the narrow genre of techno-thrillers, the novel still explains ordnance with the avidity that Judith Krantz devotes to designer labels. There are also a few mawkish passages: "Clark embraced Ryan in the way that men do only with their wives, their children and those with whom they have faced death."

Best-selling novels are often bedeviled by potboiler reputations, and Clancy echoes a familiar lament when he says, "It is disconcerting that the critics don't think of thriller writers as serious writers." In fairness, he should not be dismissed as merely another book-biz commodity, the action-adventure counterpart to Danielle Steel or Sidney Sheldon. For one thing, Clancy's narrative prose rarely descends to the all too familiar level of "I'm dictating as fast as I can." More important, to measure Clancy's output solely in terms of bookstore Q-Ratings and royalty statements would be to distort the moral seriousness that undergirds his fiction. Clancy believes passionately in professionalism, preserving order, patriotism and playing by the rules. As Ryan says to the President near the end of the novel, "Sir, the oath our people take when they put the uniform on requires them to bear 'true faith and allegiance' to their country. Isn't it written down somewhere that the country owes them the same thing?"

AN AMERICAN HERO

Little more than six years ago, Tom Clancy was spending every spare moment at the dining-room table composing his first novel on an IBM Selectric that he lugged home from the office. His wife Wanda, who had just given birth to a son, brooded over his neglect of his insurance business, and his two daughters balked at having to eat all their meals off TV trays. But Clancy saw his writing as a way to climb out of "the middle-class trap."

When it came to creating a pedigree for his alter ego, Jack Ryan, Clancy made certain that he came equipped with the fiscal independence that the author so painfully lacked. Near the beginning of *Red October*, Clancy wrote, "[Ryan] was not afraid to speak his mind. Part of that came from having money and being married to more money . . . Ryan could not be bought, bribed or bullied."

These days, the study alone of Clancy's new eight-bedroom dream house overlooking the Chesapeake Bay in Huntingtown, Md., is larger than the Calvert County insurance agency that he escaped from. And what home boasts such self-indulgent extras as Clancy's private underground pistol range? "When I set up the background for Jack Ryan," Clancy recalls. "I gave him everything I thought one could possibly need in life." But this study can serve as an index of the author's own wish list. There are toys (a pool table), tools (a MacIntosh computer), tributes (five director's chairs from the film set of *Red October*) and tokens that symbolize Clancy's embrace by the U.S. military (the bookshelves are punctuated by upwards of 80 souvenir caps bearing logos like USS CASIMIR PULASKI). Looking around the room, Clancy laughs, as much to himself as anyone else: "Now I have more than Jack Ryan." Following the up-from-nowhere success of *Red October*, Clancy, who was dropped from the ROTC program at Loyola College because of severe myopia, quickly became the Navy's favorite houseguest. Captain J. Michael Rodgers, who commanded the destroyer squadron in which Clancy first went to sea aboard the U.S.S. Gallery, puts it this way: "The Aeneid begins, 'I sing of arms and the man.' In that tradition, Tom is our minstrel."

That voyage not only launched a friendship between Rodgers and Clancy, a fellow classicist, but it also gave the novelist a new vocational dream. "I've told my friends in the Navy for five years now, I would trade what I do to be a commanding officer of a ship," Clancy says. One could almost see him standing on deck, a tall, sandy-haired C.O., wearing dark glasses and an intense expression. "As I get a little older, I get further away from it, but command of a ship is probably the best job in the world."

PUBLIC ACCESS

Many in the Pentagon were stunned by the accuracy of *Red October.* "When I first met Clancy at a White House lunch," recalls former Navy Secretary John Lehman, "I joked that if he had been a naval officer, I would have had him court-martialed; the book revealed that much that had been classified about antisubmarine warfare. Of course, nobody for a moment suspected him of getting access to classified information."

Clancy prides himself on the verisimilitude of the technical details in his novels, but insists that his methodology is simple: "It's amazing what you can get from the public press." Yet in conversation, Clancy can also purport to be privy to more than a layman's share of sensitive information, thanks to his legion of admirers in the military. At times, he will break off an anecdote by saying, "It's a shame that I can't tell you about that."

Surprisingly, Clancy claims to have researched *Danger* in less than a week. He felt no compulsion to visit Colombia, since he subscribes to the you've-seen-one-jungle-you've-seen-them-all philosophy. Clancy finds it routine that he learned all that he needed to know about the Army's light-fighters during a three-day visit to Fort Ord, Calif. "A warrior is a warrior," Clancy insists, using a favorite term of praise, "whether they're light infantrymen, submariners, fighter pilots or whatever. The way they express themselves may be different, but the personality types are pretty much the same."

Clancy has been at loose ends since he came down from the adrenaline rush of completing *Danger* (he wrote the final 45 manuscript pages in a single day to meet his May 1 deadline). His self-reward was a cross-country train trip with wife Wanda and their four children (the youngest is a three-year-old daughter), plus Rodgers and his wife. Clancy, who shares his hero Ryan's aversion to flying, rented an entire Amtrak parlor car for the trip.

LIFE AFTER BOOKS

Clancy has resisted signing a new book contract with his publisher, Putnam, "because I don't want all the pressure over me, the delivery date and all that stuff." Even though he talks boldly about taking an entire year off "to do something different," Wanda predicts that his sabbatical will not last another two months. Over the summer, Clancy has already been tinkering with three different books—a new Ryan tale, a World War II naval adventure and a half-completed novel called *Without Remorse,* about a moralistic CIA assassin named Clark. Clancy's rationale for his new spate of writing: "You just can't sit at the computer and stare at the blank screen." But such frenetic activity cannot dispel the persistent sense that Clancy is grappling with his own form of mid-life crisis: the dilemma posed by answered prayers. "Tom is doing what you and I would do when we achieve a goal," says Lieut. Commander Gerry Carroll, a Navy pilot who has been Clancy's close friend since high school. "He's asking himself. 'Now what should I try to do?' It's not the great American ennui in the sense of a mystified now-what. It's more of an earnestness to hitch up your wagon and get on to the next horizon."

For Clancy, the beckoning horizon has long been Government service. He is still enough of an earnest outsider to recall each of his seven visits to the White House (the most recent: in March, to watch a screening of *New York Stories* with George H.W. Bush). But ever since Ronald Reagan stepped forward as Clancy's First Reader, the author has had more reason than most to muse about the what-ifs of being officially on the inside.

In April [1989] he was asked to serve as an unpaid consultant to the National Space Council, chaired by Vice President Dan Quayle. Although Clancy is still negotiating the wording of the standard nondisclosure agreement so it does not impede future novels, his eagerness to serve is palpable. "They wouldn't have asked me in if they didn't think I'd be useful." he says, the hope almost audible in his voice. But the novelist can also sound like Ryan when he declares. "Somebody in my position has the unique ability to look an official in the eye and says, 'What you just said is garbage.'" But the Bush team has other ideas. "What we had in mind," says an Administration insider, "is tapping his expertise in creating public enthusiasm for the space program."

Novelists can become captives of their own Walter Mitty fantasies (remember Norman Mailer's political career?). It may be Clancy's entrée to the powerful that now encourages him to aspire to something beyond the National Space Council. For although he has no formal military or national-security credentials, what he privately covets is nothing less than Ryan's job as deputy director (intelligence) of the CIA. It may be only an armchair ambition, but at moments he seriously weighs whether he could handle the challenge. "I think I would be pretty good at it," he muses. "Maybe I could find out someday if I'm as smart as I say I am."

That self-confident veneer is vintage Clancy. "I don't think Tom believes there's anything on this planet that he can't do," says Carroll. But even if he never gets to test his talents in government, Clancy has already performed a national service of sorts: more than any recent popular novelist he has sought to explain the military and its moral code to civilians. Such a voice was needed, for Viet Nam had created a barrier of estrangement between America's warrior class and the nation it serves. Tom Clancy's novels may be romanticized, but they have helped bring down this wall. Not bad for a small-town insurance man who thought he might try his hand at popular fiction.

Tom Clancy Understands the American Psyche

Jason Cowley

Jason Cowley says that Tom Clancy is the novelist who comes closest to understanding the American psyche: paranoid, isolated, and confrontational. Cowley witnessed an address that Clancy made at the Ministry of Defense where the popular author launched into a rant on the nature of warfare, steeped in anti-Communist and anti-Islamic sentiment. Cowley asserted that Clancy's immense popularity could certainly be attributed to his ability to target an enemy, and offer a convincing and simple solution to a problem as complex as terrorism. Cowley feels that it is not always Clancy's opinion that everyone could agree on, but the nature of his personality to take a stance, however controversial, and defend it wholeheartedly that makes him such a spectacle to take notice of. Cowley concludes that Clancy's popularity is somewhat enigmatic because it doesn't hinge on how well liked he or his novels are, but rather how omnipresent his name is as a force inside and outside the realm of mass-market fiction.

Jason Cowley writes for the *New Statesman*, a weekly magazine with an online counterpart.

Long before the devastating attacks on New York and Washington [on September 11, 2001], America seemed haunted by a strange and persistent melancholy, even in the midst of spectacular superabundance. Searching for secular redemption, modern Americans long to become engines of their own self-creation, freed from any taint of the past. But Americans are prisoners of their own achievement, never able to reach the limits of their ever-proliferating desires. What remains is hideous boredom.

Modern America, for all its professed religiosity, is in thrall to a peculiar nihilism; it is essentially an entertainment culture, addicted to narratives of catastrophe. American video games, disaster movies and concept thrillers have long been sustained by eschatological anxiety. From an early age, children are taught to fear the end of America itself, the destruction by malign forces of all that is held most true. Once, these forces came from outer space, later, from behind the Iron Curtain, carrying an atheistic date stamp. Today, they come from the Islamic world—and they have never been more threatening. No one exploits American fears of, and unconscious longing for, catastrophe more expertly than the concept-thriller writer Tom Clancy, said to be the highest-paid author in the world (his recent two-book deal is worth a reported $45m). Clancy is a cultural phenomenon: arguably the most popular novelist on earth, with more than 30 million of his books in print, an unreconstructed Republican hawk and a close friend of the Reagan family and Oliver North [American implicated in Iran-contra hearings]. 'If you don't like driving a tank, there's something wrong with you,' Clancy once said. His work is saturated with research and hard detail; his descriptions of nuclear submarines and fighter jets have a startling authenticity—the boffin porn of the teenage defence electronics fanatic. ['A lot of what I know about warfare I learnt from reading Tom,' said Colin Powell, the U.S. secretary of state and former chairman of the joint chiefs of staff.]

THE MODERN AMERICAN PSYCHE

To read Clancy, then, is to understand why so many Americans wish to withdraw behind a virtual defensive shield, leaving themselves free to wander overlit shopping malls of limitless mediocrity, in isolation from a crazy world. In Clancy's books, the world is always close to or at war and the US is threatened with extinction. 'Is this the promised end?' asks Kent in *King Lear.* 'Or,' replies Edgar, 'image of that horror?' Through reading Clancy, Americans have lived vicariously with a sense of an ending, simultaneously embracing what they most fear and perhaps most desire—the ruin of cities, the collapse of nations, the vanquishing of alien peoples. Clancy may not yet have shown them the promised end (though he has come close), but he has repeatedly shown them images of that horror: assassination and the collapse of skyscrapers; battles at sea, on land and in the sky; perpetual conflict in the Middle East; and, most poignantly, the hijacking by Arab militants of civilian planes so that they may be used as lethal weapons against the American people (*The Sum of All Fears*, 1991). These images of horror have been replicated endlessly in Hollywood movies and in computer games, so that it is no exaggeration to describe Clancy as the novelist who comes closest to understanding and animating the modern American psyche: paranoid, deluded, isolated and aggressively confrontational.

THE CLANCY EMPIRE

Clancy has become his own global brand. He has franchised out his name to a team of ghost-writers who produce, under the 'Op-Center' consortium, books that are bestsellers but have none of the lustre or huge narrative momentum of his own techno-thrillers. Hollywood agents scramble to buy the multimillion-dollar film rights to his books, including *Patriot Games*, which was about a plot by the IRA to murder the British royal family and starred Harrison Ford as Clancy's all-action hero Jack Ryan; and *The Hunt for Red October*, which featured Sean Connery in a story about a rogue Soviet nuclear submarine. Clancy also owns Red Storm Entertainment, a software company that creates video games from the material of his fiction and which, he believes, will enable him to create a 'new art form'. 'Instead of telling them to people as you do if you're a playwright or an author, we present the reader with stories in which he can participate.'

Acute myopia prevented Clancy from joining the armed forces. The wound still festers and perhaps explains why he is often photographed in military clothing and why he parked a tank on the front lawn of his 80-acre Maryland estate. 'I wanted to serve my couple of years as a lieutenant,' he said. 'I just thought I owed that to my country. But they didn't want me; that's the name of the game.' The heroes of his novels are men (they are always men) of action, monoliths of courage and self-affirmation. They have right on their side, and if you are not for them, you are against them. This is a fictional world of simple and incisive oppositions, a binary realm of good and bad, black and white, right and wrong.

The son of a postman from Baltimore, Clancy was working as a door-to-door insurance salesman when he began work on his first novel. It was not published until 1985, when he was 38, and then only quietly, without marketing or advertising. Yet its analysis of cold-war geopolitics and portrayal of nuclear submarine technology was so accurate as to prompt accusations that he had seen classified documents. Within a year, he was a millionaire, delivering lectures to the US National War College and meeting regularly at the White House with Ronald Reagan, still described by Clancy as 'America's greatest president'.

In person, Clancy is big, swaggering, deep-voiced and straight-backed—the John Wayne of fiction. He speaks in rapid, staccato sentences, studded with aphorisms and gnomic utterances. With his thick, dark, steel-framed spectacles, he resembles a highway cop, or perhaps a hitman. The blue smoke from his constant cigarette spirals and curls.

PRIMARY SOURCE

I first met him at the National Liberal Club in Whitehall, when he was visiting London to address the monthly forum of senior naval staff at the Ministry of Defence. Dressed in their lounge suits, the men from the Royal Navy filed sombrely into the club, huddling together beneath a bust of [World War I British prime minister] Lloyd George. It was a perfectly English occasion, whisperingly conspiratorial and clubbable. Then Clancy strode into the room, accompanied by an alarmingly tall blonde woman whose big, buoyant hair had all the elaborate intricacy of a wasp's nest (Clancy had recently separated from his wife of more than 20 years). The mood was transformed. Captain Peter Hoare, the head of defence studies in the Royal Navy, introduced Clancy by saying that he needed 'no introduction'. Clancy nodded approvingly, stubbed out his cigarette and, to the accompaniment of polite laughter, said: 'I've never been in a liberal club before. I'm a conservative.'

PUBLIC PERSONA

From there, speaking without notes, he delivered his theory of warfare, steeped in anticommunist and anti-Islamic sentiment. He roamed restlessly across centuries and offered potted histories of the great battles in an engaging, wised-up vernacular. It was an aggressive, bravura performance that left much of his audience shifting with patrician unease. Although the forum was private and nothing was to be reported, a worried Captain Hoare rang me the next day. He wanted to reiterate that nothing Clancy had said was 'official naval policy; I thought he was going to talk about how his thrillers have enhanced the reputation of the US military'.

After his talk, Clancy and I met for a drink, during which he launched more assaults on liberals, the French, Hollywood ('giving your book to Hollywood is like turning your daughter over to a pimp'), the CIA, Islamic fundamentalists, Marxist-Leninists and Bill Clinton. He told me about what he called the 'Ryan doctrine' of warfare, named after the hero of his novels. 'The Ryan doctrine is about taking out the principal enemy. What you do is drop four or five SAS [Special Air Service]-style guys into, say, Iraq, guys who can disappear in an instant, speak the language, have the moustaches and funny gear—you know, the hats and clothes. What they do is use ground laser designators to track and locate Saddam. Then bang, you strike from the air. The good guys win again.'

IS CLANCY CREDIBLE?

It all sounded so simple. Some, no doubt, will say that Clancy speaks with the robust common sense of the ordinary American, of which President G.W. Bush is undoubtedly one (except for the good fortune of his birth). Listening to Bush struggling to articulate the nature of his hurt, humiliation and outrage, and his stumbling attempts to offer sympathy and leadership to a traumatised nation, I have thought often of Clancy and his Ryan doctrine of warfare. 'To me, the Ryan doctrine is the logical extension of military technology,' Clancy told me. 'Killing people doesn't worry me so long as you have a good enough reason. The Ryan doctrine gives you a reason.' As do irrational messianic fervour (Bin Laden) and wounded indignation (George Bush).

To Clancy, war is the 'ultimate blood sport': to deny its necessity is to deny the truth. His career as a writer may have been one long, extended patriot game, but as his country prepares to strike against a nameless and opaque enemy, he must be horrified at how adeptly Islamic terrorists appropriated the destructive impulses of American entertainment culture, making of a nation's apocalyptic fantasies a terrifying actuality, as if they were attempting to speak to Americans in their own language. In so doing, the terrorists created instantly replicable images of catastrophe that will haunt our imaginings for ever, not least those of Tom Clancy himself, who for so long has animated our anxieties, dramatised our disasters and savoured our last moments. Except that even he could not have been prepared for what happened next—for apocalypse here and now, in New York [September 11, 2001].

Why Tom Clancy Is Popular

Marc A. Cerasini

Marc A. Cerasini examines what makes Tom Clancy's
work so popular. Cerasini contends that Clancy's techno-
thrillers are not actually unique, so this quality cannot explain the books' success. The real explanation for Clancy's
success is the generally positive outlook reflected in his
novels. While many techno-thriller writers must operate
under the assumption that war is a necessary and innate
human institution, Cerasini commends Tom Clancy for
his attempt to portray future wars as conventional, rather
than glorifying and exploiting a nuclear, apocalyptic war.
Cerasini also feels that Clancy's positivity bleeds into his
portrayal of the U.S. military, which comes off as nothing
less than benevolent and heroic in each novel, is reflected
in his novels is his generally positive outlook.

Tom Clancy firmly believes that America's system of
democratic values provides the tools necessary for an individual in a society to exercise his or her freedom to its
fullest potential. Much of Clancy's immediate success is
that he stands behind America, and expresses its role as a
force of justice on the international stage in a positive way.
Cerasini feels that readers will continue to adhere to
Clancy's positivity as he embraces the United States's political system and continues to entertain us.

Marc A. Cerasini has written books on a wide array of
topics ranging from the U.S. Marine Corps Medal of
Honor winners to Star Wars and O.J. Simpson.

While it doesn't hurt to get a plug for your first novel from
one of the most popular presidents of this century, Ronald
Reagan's admiration for Clancy's *The Hunt for Red October*

Marc A. Cerasini, "Why Tom Clancy?" *The Tom Clancy Companion*, edited by
Martin H. Greenburg. New York: Berkley Books, 1992. Copyright © 1992 by Jack
Ryan Enterprises, Ltd. Reproduced by permission of the publisher.

doesn't reach far enough to explain the phenomenal popularity of Clancy's fiction. Since his first novel went into Berkley paperback, each of Clancy's subsequent novels has outsold the previous ones, marking a steady rise in the popularity of this remarkable author.

What are this author's singular accomplishments? What makes Tom Clancy's work unique?

As we have seen, Clancy fused the traditional thriller/espionage genre with elements of science fiction such as preoccupation with technology and a futurist's vision of political events on the near horizon, to produce the techno-thriller. But, as the author himself has complained when asked about the technological aspects of his fiction, "Why doesn't anyone talk about techno-mysteries?" That is, why stress Clancy's use of technology, since it is neither unique in contemporary fiction nor as pervasive in the author's work as we are led to believe.

Clancy's vision of future warfare is one of his most enduring achievements. Of all the author's work, *Red Storm Rising* is the most imitated, and this particular novel has given birth to a sub-genre of its own, practiced by authors from Larry Bond to Ralph Peters to Payne Harrison. His vision of futuristic warfare is nothing new. We have seen that near-future, imaginary war novels, as envisioned by authors like William Le Queux and H.G. Wells, were popular during the decades preceding the First World War. Clancy merely updated this classic subgenre of science fiction and portrayed a *conventional* war when everyone else seemed to be thinking *nuclear* war.

Clancy's grasp of current affairs on the international scene is probably also an important factor in his popularity. The tide of international events occurring during the last decade has been unmatched since the Second World War, and we should of course be aware of the revolutionary changes sweeping the world. But since when does a careful analysis of current events guarantee the appeal of a work of fiction?

I think we have to look a little more deeply at Clancy's novels to find the reasons for his audience appeal.

CLANCY BEHIND AMERICA

The real secret of Tom Clancy's popularity, I believe, is his deeply held personal and political philosophy, which is reflected in his novels, and the fact that the author prefers to emphasize positives over negatives. Four factors that I believe are vital to his appeal are: (1) his positive portrayal of the United States of America and the political system we enjoy, (2) his positive portrayal of the American military and intelligence agencies, (3) his belief that political and military might can be used for the good of humanity and are not innately evil, and, (4) the fact that the author presents positive male role-models in his fiction, running counter to the fashion in popular literature for the last twenty or so years.

Tom Clancy loves freedom. He is not naive about the problems our society faces, and will continue to face in the future, but he is confident that our enlightened system of Western democratic values provides the tools we need to remedy social or political problems. Rather than blame America, Clancy sees our nation as a beacon and a leader in the decades and perhaps centuries to come, as a force for justice in an unjust world. This is a vision that is vital if America is going to assume its role in the international community and do the job only Americans—because of our unique freedoms and our impressive wealth—can accomplish. The new world order cannot be born without the active intervention of the United States.

Clancy's reversal of the trend, so fashionable in the media, in popular fiction, and among the intelligentsia, of bashing the "military-industrial complex" and the intelligence agencies is a big factor in his appeal. Besides the obvious point that many, many Americans work in these areas and may not like being blamed for the ills of the world, we must remember that we need our military. When the military is called to duty, it responds and does what it is ordered to do by the Commander in Chief. And we must not forget that all Americans are potential soldiers, that we are a nation of citizen-soldiers, and, in principle, do not make war without the will and consent of the people of the United States.

The fiction of Tom Clancy and his peers did the world a service by paving the way for Operation Desert Shield, then Desert Storm. The shift in public opinion regarding the use of the military can be traced in part to the popularity of the techno-thriller genre, which educated us about the weapons, the strategies, and the very nature of modern warfare.

WILL TOM CLANCY'S WORK ENDURE?

Probably. His fiction is certainly not frozen in time, and continues to grow and mature. Although some of his early novels may someday appear dated, Clancy continues to explore new territory and will always remain current—if not well ahead of his time. But even the works that appear to be dated will provide future generations with a clear picture of the crucial period in history that marked the beginning of the end of Marxist-Leninist rule in the Soviet Union and the birth of the new world order. And Tom Clancy will find new areas to explore, new ways to challenge us through his fiction, and new ways to entertain us in the grand manner we have come to expect from this talented and thoughtful author.

For Further Research

Fiction by Tom Clancy

The Bear and the Dragon. New York: G.P. Putnam's Sons, 2000.

The Cardinal of the Kremlin. New York: G.P. Putnam's Sons, 1988.

Clear and Present Danger. New York: G.P. Putnam's Sons, 1989.

Debt of Honor. New York: G.P. Putnam's Sons, 1994.

Executive Orders. New York: G.P. Putnam's Sons, 1996.

The Hunt for Red October. Annapolis: Naval Institute Press, 1984.

Patriot Games. New York: G.P. Putnam's Sons, 1987.

Rainbow Six. New York: G.P. Putnam's Sons, 1997.

Red Rabbit. New York: G.P. Putnam's Sons, 2002.

Red Storm Rising. New York: G.P. Putnam's Sons, 1986.

The Sum of All Fears. New York: G.P. Putnam's Sons, 1991.

Without Remorse. New York: G.P. Putnam's Sons, 1993.

Nonfiction by Tom Clancy

Airborne. New York: Berkley Books, 1997.

Carrier. New York: Berkley Books, 1999.

Every Man a Tiger. New York: Berkley Books, 1999.

Into the Storm: A Study in Command. New York: Berkley Books, 1997.

Marine. New York: Berkley Books, 1996.

SSN: Strategies of Submarine Warfare. New York: Berkley Books, 1996.

Submarine. New York: Berkley Books, 1993.

Tom Clancy's Op-Center Series

Tom Clancy's Op-Center. Created by Tom Clancy and Steve Pieczenik. New York: Berkley Books, 1995.

Tom Clancy's Op-Center: Acts of War. Created by Tom Clancy and Steve Pieczenik. New York: Berkley Books, 1996.

Tom Clancy's Op-Center: Balance of Power. Created by Tom Clancy and Steve Pieczenik. New York: Berkley Books, 1998.

Tom Clancy's Op-Center: Divide and Conquer. Created by Tom Clancy and Steve Pieczenik. New York: Berkley Books, 2000.

Tom Clancy's Op-Center: Games of State. Created by Tom Clancy and Steve Pieczenik. New York: Berkley Books, 1996.

Tom Clancy's Op-Center: Line of Control. Created by Tom Clancy and Steve Pieczenik. New York: Berkley Books, 2001.

Tom Clancy's Op-Center: Mirror Image. Created by Tom Clancy and Steve Pieczenik. New York: Berkley Books, 1995.

Tom Clancy's Op-Center: Mission of Honor. Created by Tom Clancy and Steve Pieczenik. New York: Berkley Books, 2002.

Tom Clancy's Op-Center: State of Siege. Created by Tom Clancy and Steve Pieczenik. New York: Berkley Books, 1999.

Net Force Series

Net Force. Tom Clancy, Steve Pieczenik. New York: Berkley Books, 1998.

Net Force 2: Hidden Agendas. Tom Clancy, Steve Pieczenik. New York: Berkley Books, 1999.

Net Force 3: Night Moves. Tom Clancy, Steve Pieczenik. New York: Berkley Books, 2000.

Net Force 4: Breaking Point. Tom Clancy, Steve Pieczenik. New York: Berkley Books, 2000.

Net Force 5: Point of Impact. Steve Perry with Tom Clancy and Steve Pieczenik. New York: Berkley Books, 2001.

Net Force 6: End Game. Diane Duane with Tom Clancy and Steve Pieczenik. New York: Berkley Books, 1999.

Net Force 7: State of War. Steve Perry with Tom Clancy and Steve Pieczenik. New York: Berkley Books, 2003.

Net Force 8: Shadow of Honor. Mel Odom with Tom Clancy and Steve Pieczenik. New York: Berkley Books, 2000.

Net Force 9: Private Lives. Bill McCay with Tom Clancy and Steve Pieczenik. New York: Berkley Books, 2000.

Net Force 10: Safe House. Diane Duane with Tom Clancy and Steve Pieczenik. New York: Berkley Books, 2000.

Net Force 11: Gameprey. Mel Odom with Tom Clancy and Steve Pieczenik. New York: Berkley Books, 2000.

Net Force 13: Deathworld. Diane Duane with Tom Clancy and Steve Pieczenik. New York: Berkley Books, 2000.

Net Force 14: High Wire. Mel Odom with Tom Clancy and Steve Pieczenik. New York: Berkley Books, 2001.

Net Force 15: Cold Case. Tom Clancy. New York: Berkley Books, 2001.

Net Force 16: Runaways. Diane Duane with Tom Clancy and Steve Pieczenik. New York: Berkley Books, 2001.

Net Force 17: Cloak and Dagger. Mel Odom with Tom Clancy and Steve Pieczenik. New York: Berkley Books, 2003.

Works About Tom Clancy

Warren Berger, "Clear and Present Danger; Touring Ground Zero with Tom Clancy," *Book,* January/February 2002, pp. 55–57.

Tom Clancy and Russel Seitz, "Five Minutes Past Midnight," *National Interest,* Winter 1991, pp. 3–12.

John Donnelly, "Hot Under the Epaulets," *Salon,* June 1997. www.salonmagazine.com.   .

Helen S. Garson, *Tom Clancy: A Critical Companion.* Westport, CT: Greenwood Press, 1996.

Martin Greenburg, *The Tom Clancy Companion.* New York: Berkley Books, 1992.

Jean Ross, "Tom Clancy," *Contemporary Authors,* vol. 131. Detroit: Gale Research, 1991.

Evan Thomas, "The Art of the Techno-Thriller," *Newsweek,* August 8, 1988.

Cynthia Ward, "Author Tom Clancy and His Novels in Defense of America," *Conservative Digest,* April 1988.

Jeff Zaleski, "The Hunt for Tom Clancy," *Publishers Weekly,* July 13, 1998.

Websites

Doppler's Tom Clancy Page, www.quis.net. Contains links to other sites devoted to Tom Clancy and his works. Selected essays on some of Clancy's works can be accessed through this site.

Tom Clancy FAQ, www.clancyfaq.com. This website provides a forum for a discussion of Tom Clancy himself, his books, films based on his books, and games Clancy has inspired. Links to other sites of interest to Clancy fans are included.

Tom Clancy Web Files, http://users.cybercity.dk. A fan-maintained site features information on some of Tom Clancy's books, films, and games. A brief biography of the author is included.

INDEX